THE
WICKED WIT OF
SCOTLAND

THE
WICKED WIT OF
SCOTLAND

ROD GREEN

MICHAEL O'MARA BOOKS LIMITED

First published in Great Britain in 2018 by
Michael O'Mara Books Limited
9 Lion Yard
Tremadoc Road
London SW4 7NQ

A CIP catalogue record for this book is available from the British
Library.

Papers used by Michael O'Mara Books Limited are natural, recyclable
products made from wood grown in sustainable forests. The
manufacturing processes conform to the environmental regulations of
the country of origin.

ISBN: 978-1-78929-022-6 in hardback print format
ISBN: 978-1-78929-032-5 in ebook format

1 2 3 4 5 6 7 8 9 10

Designed and typeset by Design 23
Illustrations by Andrew Pinder

Printed and bound by CPI Group (UK) Ltd, Croydon, CR0 4YY
www.mombooks.com

CONTENTS

INTRODUCTION

Some people think that the Scots are miserable, dour and dreich, a bit like our weather. They point to Andy Murray as a typically morose Scotsman droning away with a flat, monotone delivery – a low-pitched whine that's as annoying as an inflating bagpipe. But how would you feel if you had just spent five hours thundering around a tennis court opposite Novak Djokovic . . . and lost? When Murray won gold for Great Britain at the 2012 Olympic Games, he was feted as a national (British) hero, yet still the doom-mongers wouldn't leave him alone. 'It'll make a change,' read one online comment, 'to have someone more miserable than the Queen on our stamps.'

That is hugely unfair. Neither Andy nor the Queen are miserable. They both have the wonderful Scottish sense of humour. Andy has it from Monday to Wednesday and the Queen takes it back for the rest of the week. How else could Andy have put up with comedian Michael McIntyre invading his hotel room in the middle of the night to force him to take part in a challenge for Sport Relief? Andy swore, laughed, joined in the fun and even sang Spice Girls' songs with ex-Ginger Spice, Geri Halliwell. And the Queen? The Scots claim her as Scottish, of course, as her mother was Scottish and she spends several weeks during the summer at Balmoral. You might say she is only half-Scottish and the rest is some strange Anglo-German mix, but as you go through this book you will find that we Scots don't give a hoot about half measures. Half-Scottish is Scottish as far as we are concerned because the Scottish portion will stand head and shoulders above all the rest.

We will claim anything we can as Scottish. So if it's even a wee bit Scottish, it's Scottish; whether it's the invention of the steam engine, the first man on the Moon or Her Majesty The Queen – who has a fine sense of humour, by the way. While meeting and greeting on a walkabout in Scotland, she turned a corner only to bump into someone who had no idea the Queen was in the neighbourhood and who remarked, 'You look just like the Queen …!' to which the Queen replied, 'How reassuring.'

Once something has been claimed as Scottish, it is Scottish for ever. We make things ours by cat-marking them with a tartan-scented spray that never washes off. Golf was probably invented in Holland but we decided we'd have that years ago. Sprayed Scottish – golf is ours. Bagpipes evolved in the Middle East and have existed all over Europe for many centuries. Sprayed Scottish – bagpipes are ours. Whisky was almost certainly distilled in Ireland long before we got hold of it. Sprayed Scottish – whisky is ours. As comedian Chic Murray put it: 'A Scot is a man who keeps the Sabbath, and everything else he can lay his hands on.'

Chic Murray touched on one of the most famous traits of Scottishness – a grasping meanness that has earned us the reputation of being as tight as two coats of paint. In the United States, where there are so many people of Scots descent and where so many Scots have played such a huge role in the evolution of the nation that the whole country is practically a suburb of Glasgow, they like to say that their Grand Canyon was started by a Scotsman who lost a dime in a ditch.

In Scotland, we embrace all of the mocking stereotypes – the images of mean Scots, drunken Scots, aggressive Scots, unintelligible Scots, ginger-bearded, kilt-wearing, bagpipe-playing, bar-brawling, haggis-eating, caber-tossing, whisky-sozzled Scots. Bring them all on. We love to laugh at them as much as anyone else because we know that none of them are true. Well, most of them aren't true. Well, some of them are at least a bit exaggerated. We all love stories about the Scotsman who says he's just washed his kilt and he can't do a fling with it. We've all heard people pointing out that the difference between bagpipes and a trampoline is that eventually you get tired of jumping on a trampoline.

We love those jokes and we hear them all the time when we are outside Scotland. There's a funny thing about living abroad, which includes living in England, the locals think that you have a really broad Scots accent. It is easy for a Scotsman to retain his accent because we never give anything away, after all. So the locals think we have strong Scottish accents and ask us to say ridiculous things like 'purple burglar alarm'. Then they fall about laughing. We know that the laugh is really on them because they can't enunciate properly, unlike us Scots. And there is no shortage of Scots abroad for people to pick on. There are far more of us living elsewhere than there are in Scotland. In London, some say it is a disgrace that there are so many dim-witted Scots living rough on the streets. The Scots like to think that this helps to raise the average IQ both in Scotland and in London.

Holding on to your accent when you are away from home doesn't seem difficult until you go back to Scotland and everyone asks why you're speaking like a foreigner, the classic comment being, 'You've been so long in England even Lulu's got a better accent than you!' Returning to Scotland when you've been away for a while can be a risky business, too. In some areas north of the border, the average male life expectancy is up to ten years less than that in southern England, and you wouldn't want to get caught out while you're there, would you?

The real reason, however, that most Scots living in exile don't go back to Scotland as much as they should is that each time they go back it becomes a little more difficult to leave again. Scotland is, after all, the most wonderful country on the face of the planet.

This book takes a look at some of the things that make Scotland and the Scots peculiarly Scottish. It includes lots of true stories, some not-so-true stories, some apocryphal tales, some downright fabrications and some jokes that prove we Scots are the most miserable, joyous, introverted, gregarious, talentless, gifted, dim-witted, intelligent, lazy, industrious, scowly, smiley people in the world. And do we have a sense of humour? Of course we do – it's free, isn't it?

CHAPTER ONE

THE SHAPE
OF THINGS

In Scotland, I think everyone would agree that the geography of the country shapes not only its physical boundaries and national identity, but also the character of its people. The people of Glasgow called Edinburgh 'The Far East', although it is less than fifty miles away, and the people of Edinburgh called Glasgow 'The Wild West'. As Glaswegian comedian Kevin Bridges said, 'Edinburgh and Glasgow – same country, two very different cities.'

PIPE DREAMS

Musician Jack Bruce, who played bass with Eric Clapton and Ginger Baker in the celebrated British supergroup Cream, knew hard times as a youngster in Glasgow, but he had a clear idea of what he wanted to do. 'I wanted to write great tunes, play the bass, be a band leader, and smoke a big funny pipe like Charlie Mingus,' he said, 'so I went out and bought the pipe when I was around eighteen or nineteen years old. You know, even women smoked a pipe in Glasgow.'

A talented musician, Bruce studied cello and composition at Glasgow's Royal Scottish Academy of Music and Drama, but would never have been able to do so without scholarship funding. 'Growing up in inner-city Glasgow,' he said, 'it sometimes seemed to me money hadn't been invented.'

'The Scots are a very tough people. They have drive-by headbuttings. In Glasgow, a sweatband is considered a silencer.'

EMO PHILIPS

GLASGOW'S MILES BETTER

In 1983, Glasgow launched a PR campaign to rebrand itself and change people's perceptions of the city. Instead of a hard-drinking, violent town, the Lord Provost wanted to promote Glasgow in the same way that the 'I Love New York' campaign, using the heart symbol – I ♥ New York – had changed New York's image. He wanted something smiley and happy. The result was the slogan 'Glasgow's Miles Better', using an image of Roger Hargreaves' Mr Men character, Mr Happy. One copywriter's suggestion, rejected at an early brainstorming session, was 'Glasgow – Come For A Laugh, Leave In Stitches'.

'When Glasgow was made the Cultural Capital of Europe, the inhabitants' reaction was very healthy. They became terrified that it would put 20p on the price of a pint of bitter.'

JEFFREY BERNARD

LIGHT REFLECTIONS

Actor Brian Cox was brought up in Dundee and has had a remarkable career, working with the Royal Shakespeare Company and appearing in Hollywood movies as diverse as *The Bourne Supremacy* and *Troy*. In 2012, he filmed the BBC TV comedy series *Bob Servant* in Glasgow and also Broughty Ferry, a Dundee suburb nestling at the mouth of the River Tay in eastern Scotland. 'There's so much light in Broughty Ferry,' he said, reflecting (almost literally) on the difference between the west and east coasts of Scotland. 'I think the humour in Glasgow is darker because it's so much more gloomy. There's a perpetual misery there.'

'Before you judge a man, walk a mile in his shoes. After that, who cares? He's a mile away and you have his shoes.'

BILLY CONNOLLY

THE GLASWEGIAN SOLUTION

At a U2 concert in Glasgow, lead singer Bono had a point to make. He asked the audience for total silence, and the audience duly obeyed. Then, he began slowly clapping his hands, one clap every few seconds. The Glaswegian audience remained totally silent and, after a series of these deliberately timed handclaps, Bono announced, 'Every time I clap my hands, a child in Africa dies.'

And a voice from the front row shouted, 'Well, stop clapping then, ye evil bastard!'

'Las Vegas and Glasgow have a lot in common. They're the only two places in the world where you can pay for sex with chips.'

FRANKIE BOYLE

'My childhood growing up in Glasgow always sounds like some kind of sub-Catherine Cookson novel of earthy working-class immigrant life, which to some extent it was, but it wasn't really as colourful as all that.'

PETER CAPALDI

SOCKY HALL OR WILLOW VALE?

Glasgow's famous Sauchiehall Street may not be the toughest area in town, but it's a tough one to pronounce. The name probably comes from the way the street used to look when it was still quite rural. 'Sauchie' (pronounced 'socky') is from 'sauch', which means 'willow', and 'hall' derives from 'haugh', meaning 'meadow' or 'valley'. At some point 'haugh' became 'hall'. So Sauchiehall Street could easily have been the more mellow sounding Willow Meadow or Willow Vale, which seems a far more tranquil location than the following story suggests, although it does reflect the Glaswegians' undeniable talent for poking fun at themselves.

A policeman was strolling his beat along Sauchiehall Street when he spotted a man grubbing around on the pavement. 'Have you lost something?' he asked.

'Aye,' said the man, without looking up. 'I've lost my ear. Just been in a fight and got it ripped clean off.'

'Sounds like a bad lad that attacked you,' said the policeman. 'Would you recognize him again?'

'I would that,' said the man. 'I've got his nose here in my pocket.'

'Twelve highlanders and a bagpipe make a rebellion.'

SIR WALTER SCOTT

IN PRAISE OF THE CAPITAL

Edinburgh may be far smaller than Glasgow but its people are just as proud of their city by the Firth of Forth as Glaswegians are of theirs by the Clyde. Yet, for all its architectural merits, with more listed buildings than any other city outside of London and its magnificent castle sitting on top of an extinct volcano, Edinburgh's citizens have been justifiably disappointed over the years to hear the capital regularly damned with faint praise.

The city was nicknamed 'Auld Reekie' ('Auld' meaning 'Old' and 'Reekie' meaning 'Smelly') because of the smoke from its chimneys polluting the air, with Glasgow-born writer and journalist James Bone describing looking down on Edinburgh from the surrounding hills in a less than complimentary way. 'Below you lies Auld Reekie,' he wrote, 'blackened and dried, an immortal herring, "smeeked" for hundreds of years and cured in the sun.'

Writing in the nineteenth century, almost a century before Bone, Thomas Carlyle described Edinburgh as 'this accursed, stinking, reeky mass of stones and lime and dung'. Even the *Encyclopaedia Britannica*, first published in Edinburgh in 1768, could not bring itself to shower unqualified compliments on the city of its birth. 'The contrasts that make Edinburgh unique,' read the entry in the fifteenth edition, 'also make it typically Scottish, for, despite its reserved exterior, it is also a city capable of great warmth and, upon occasion, gaiety.'

Leave it to the Worst Poet in the World, William Topaz McGonagall, to pay proper tribute to Scotland's capital city:

Beautiful city of Edinburgh, most wonderful to be seen,
With your ancient palace of Holyrood and Queen's
*   Park Green,*
And your big, magnificent, elegant New College,
Where people from all nations can be taught knowledge.

'Insanity is a perfectly rational adjustment to
an insane world.'

R. D. LAING

THUNDERBIRDS ARE GO!

One of Edinburgh's most famous landmarks is the Scott Monument in Princes Street Gardens, erected in 1844 as a memorial to the great Scottish writer Sir Walter Scott. The heavily adorned Gothic spire took four years to build and stands 200 feet (61 metres) high, supported by lesser spires attached to their big sister by flying buttresses. The whole structure looks somewhat soot-blackened and grimy nowadays, but when it was first built it was pale yellowish-brown sandstone decorated with no fewer than sixty-eight statues of personalities such as Robert Burns, Lord Byron and Mary, Queen of Scots, as well as many characters from Scott's novels.

Four years after Scott died in 1832, a competition was launched to design a Gothic-style monument in his honour. The winning entry was from John Morvo, although that was not his real name. The designer was, in fact, George Meikle Kemp, who had used a pseudonym because he was not an artist or an architect but rather a humble joiner with no specialist qualifications. Nevertheless, Kemp was contracted to construct the monument, which he duly did, although he never saw it completed. On the way home from the site one foggy night in March 1844, he fell into the Union Canal and drowned. It may be as well that Kemp did not live to hear some of the comments made about his creation. Writer Charles Dickens was certainly not a fan. 'I'm sorry to report the Scott Monument a failure,' he reported, apologetic or not. 'It is like the spire of a Gothic church taken off and stuck in the ground.'

Scottish visitors to Edinburgh in the modern age have been known to peer up at the monument and say, 'It's fine and grand, but does it no' look a wee bit like Thunderbird Three?'

EDINBURGH ZOO'S MILITARY PENGUIN

Edinburgh Zoo has long been a renowned tourist attraction and, while other zoos around the world may be bigger and more glamorous, it retains many unique features that keep the visitors coming back year after year. One of those is a penguin who is an officer in the Norwegian Army. Penguins are famous for agreeing to do anything for a few handouts from a bucket of mackerel, but join the army? Really? Yes, really.

One of the zoo's king penguins (obviously no ordinary penguin would do) was first made a mascot of the Norwegian King's Guard and has since risen up the ranks from Corporal to his present-day position of Brigadier. Named Nils Olav, in 2008 he was knighted and following his investiture Sir Nils inspected an honour guard of troops. Soldiers of the Norwegian King's Guard pay him courtesy visits whenever they are in town for Edinburgh's famous Military Tattoo.

'Edinburgh shall make a delightful summer capital when we invade Britain.'

JOSEPH GOEBBELS

HOLY MOSES

Edinburgh is used to receiving high-profile visitors. It is, after all, the nation's capital and accustomed to playing host to royalty, international leaders and dignitaries of all sorts. The city likes to think that anyone who is anyone has been to Edinburgh, and if you have never been then you're a bit of a nobody. Tuck that notion away at the back of your mind and it helps to make the following story a bit more believable … but only a wee bit!

At the National Museum of Scotland in Edinburgh, a guide was showing a group of the city's schoolchildren around the Egyptian exhibits.

'And the carvings on these stones,' said the guide, 'are over three thousand years old. Moses may have seen these when he was just a wee laddie.'

'Wow!' said one of the schoolkids. 'I never knew Moses had been to Edinburgh!'

'From my experience of life I believe my personal motto should be, "Beware of men bearing flowers".'
MURIEL SPARK

THRIFTY NORTHERNERS

In the crofts, market towns and fishing villages of the far north, the legend of the Scots being careful with their cash perpetuated. There's an old story about an Aberdeen man who dropped a 50p coin and bent down so fast to pick it up that it hit him in the back of the head. Scots love these jokes. Comedian Chic Murray, who played mostly to Scottish audiences, knew how to raise a smile from the image of the thrifty Scot. 'My father was from Aberdeen, and a more generous man you couldn't wish to meet,' he said. 'I have a gold watch that belonged to him. He sold it to me on his deathbed. I wrote him a cheque for it ... post-dated of course.'

It seems that we really don't want to give up the notion of Scots being mean, even though we are the most warm-hearted, generous people you could hope to meet. Scottish music-hall artist Will Fyffe, who starred in a whole string of movies in the thirties and forties, wrote and performed many songs, one of which was 'The Spirit of a Man from Aberdeen'. The theme of the song is summed up in the following lines:

Lend me a pound
And I'll pay for drinks all round
That's the spirit of a man from Aberdeen.

In Scotland, when you eventually decide to freshen up the living room and embark on a spot of DIY, you have to be prepared to hear the joke about the man from Peterhead (even further north than Aberdeen) who stopped by his friend's house to find him methodically stripping the wallpaper.

'Doing a spot of decorating?' he enquired.

'No,' said his friend. 'We're moving house.'

'I know lads of twenty who are ninety and men of ninety who are twenty.'

A.S. NEILL

A female passenger got on the train heading north from St Andrews to Aberdeen. When the ticket collector came to inspect her ticket, he saw that it was a child's fare. He accused her of being too old to travel half-fare, but she claimed that she was still at school. Their argument raged until the train was crossing the bridge over the River Tay, at which point the ticket collector picked up the large holdall the passenger had on her lap and threatened to throw it out of the window.

'You're a monster!' yelled the woman. 'First you won't believe that I'm still at school and now you want to drown my wee boy in the river!'

'There are few more impressive sights in the world than a Scotsman on the make.'

J. M. BARRIE

EVEN UNTO DEATH

If you've been brought up on stories of 'a friend of your uncle' – never someone that the storyteller has actually met – who used to cut up old car tyres to resole his shoes, or who cycled home from work each night past a demolition site, stopped to pick up a couple of old bricks and eventually built a wall around his garden, then it makes jokes and stories about mean Scots all the more enjoyable.

This is especially true if the stories combine thriftiness with tragic and darkly morbid tales of death, such as the story about an old man, Andy McBride, who lay on his deathbed, waiting for the end to come. His breathing was shallow and weak, but his nostrils picked up the unmistakable aroma of fresh scones being baked. His favourite! Summoning all his remaining strength he lifted his head and then heaved himself out of bed. Leaning on the wall for support, he shuffled unsteadily down the corridor to the living room and nudged open the door to see the scones sitting on the table, neatly arranged on a pristine white plate.

Stumbling forward he reached out, frail and shaking, to take a scone when his wife shot out of the kitchen and smacked his hand away with a spatula. 'Keep your hands off those!' she cried. 'They're for the funeral!'

And when he finally passed away later that day, the old man's wife went to the office of the local newspaper to enquire about placing an obituary notice. The assistant explained that the notice would be charged by the word and asked the woman to write down what she wanted it to say.

The woman took a piece of paper and a pencil and wrote: 'Andy McBride died.'

'We charge by the word,' said the assistant, 'but there is a minimum charge, so you can have nine more words for the same price.'

The woman took back the piece of paper and added a few extra words so that it now read: 'Andy McBride died. Nearly new slippers and 2004 Ford Fiesta for sale.'

ISLAND LIFE

While Scots are fiercely proud to be Scottish and can draw ourselves together into a tartan horde, shoulder-to-shoulder, at the drop of a sporran should anyone who is not Scottish dare to criticize the country, we are far from a united nation. We are, perhaps, more like a family, closing ranks against hostile outsiders, yet constantly bickering with each other over things that can only really be understood if you are part of the family. Nowhere are the divisions more obvious than in the islands, where the sea creates a formidable physical barrier and the inevitable competitive family squabbles and jealousies do the rest.

Scottish islanders live among some of the most beautiful scenery on the planet, yet the islands are very demanding places to exist. People who live in Orkney and Shetland can boast that their homes are special because they are put

THE WICKED WIT OF SCOTLAND

in wee boxes all of their own at the side of the map of the rest of Scotland – and the cottage where their granny lives is just off the edge of Google maps. Whether in these far northern isles or in the Hebrides off the west coast, the isolation and sub-arctic weather mean that they need a sense of humour more than any other Scots!

WHAT'S IN A NAME?

You certainly need to be able to take a joke if you live near Shetland's Tittynans Hill or Lambhellia-cuddies. Hopefully you will have inherited a good sense of humour from whoever among your ancestors came up with the names in the first place. Fografiddle? Dud of Flamister? Steve Goldman is a mapaholic fascinated by place names and on his website, along with other gems such as 'Every road in Britain called Stephen', he has mapped some of the silliest-sounding names not only in Shetland, but in Orkney, too. Kellyan Hellyan, Tingly Loup, Grassy Cletts and Taing of the Busy are all on Orkney's islands. Take a peek at Steve's website – www.mapfodder.com – for more.

IN BLOODY ORKNEY

Legend has it that, during the Second World War, Royal Navy officer Captain Hamish Blair was stationed at Scapa Flow in Orkney and, apparently, didn't much like it. He is credited with having written a song called 'Bloody Orkney', which is a rant about the awful time he was having there:

The bloody dances make you smile,
The bloody band is bloody vile,
It only cramps your bloody style,
In bloody Orkney.

No bloody sport, no bloody games,
No bloody fun, the bloody dames
Won't even give their bloody names
In bloody Orkney.

There were a number of verses, all in much the same vein, but Orcadians appear to have had the last laugh by adding a verse of their own:

Captain Hamish 'Bloody' Blair
Isna posted here nae mare
But no-one seems to bloody care
In bloody Orkney.

Another former naval officer, who clearly had a similar view of Orkney to Captain Blair, became an actor, touring the country as Napoleon Bonaparte in a play about the French emperor. He became somewhat jaded with the twice-nightly performances and staying in grubby hotels, seeking solace with a few drams of whisky prior to going on stage. Having become somewhat over-solaced before one performance, when the captain of HMS *Northumberland* marched across the stage and confronted Napoleon with the words, 'We are taking you to St Helena', Napoleon replied, 'Take me anywhere you like as long as it's not Orkney.'

'But you have to remember, Shetland time is slower. There's a saying, that Shetland watches don't show minutes or hours – only years!'

AVALINA KRESKA, FROM HER NOVEL
THE ADDERSTANE (2016)

THE ISLANDERS' BURDEN

Just as the rest of us Scots bear the burden of our stereotypes with great good nature, so too do the islanders put up with the idea that their isolation leaves them less than worldly wise when it comes to dealing with those on the mainland. Nothing, of course, could be further from the truth and the islanders rely on staying abreast of modern technology and communications perhaps even more than the rest of us.

That, however, is never going to stand in the way of a good story about a naïve islander such as the Shetlander stranded in Edinburgh who needed to get home urgently. He phoned customer services at Edinburgh Airport to ask how long the flight to Sumburgh took:

'Just a second, sir,' said the assistant.

'That's grand,' said the islander, and he hung up.

Then there's the story about the piper from Stornoway who became disenamoured of playing in a pipe band while visiting Edinburgh and grown tired of being cruelly jeered by some tourists. Deciding that, having mastered the pipes, he could soon get the hang of pretty much any other instrument, he stormed into a music shop.

'I'd like that red saxophone, please,' he told the assistant, 'and that accordion.'

'I'm guessing that you play the pipes,' said the assistant.

'That's right,' said the piper. 'How did you know?'

'Well,' sighed the assistant, 'I can sell you the fire extinguisher, but the radiator has to stay here.'

CHAPTER TWO

NOT JUST SCOTCH MIST

If you want to experience all four seasons in a day, then Scotland is the place for you. You can start off in bright summery sunshine with blue skies on the east coast around Arbroath, then drive west into gathering clouds and falling autumnal temperatures as you wind your way through the Angus Glens before climbing into winter snow in the Cairngorms and descending into spring-like showers on the west coast.

THE WET WEST

While Scotland does have the reputation of being rainy all the time, the reality is not entirely true. Except on the west coast where it does rain constantly. The west coast of Scotland has to put up with the most rain due to the fact that the weather systems roll in off the Atlantic and for most of Scotland, especially the Outer Hebrides and northern isles, there is nothing between our shoreline and the coast of Canada except the cold, dark waters of the North Atlantic.

For the west of the country, this means that the moist air coming in from the ocean makes landfall and dumps its rain in such a way that the next shower is never far away. The wet weather and the crashing Atlantic waves have, of course, provided the weather erosion that has helped to give western Scotland some of the most dramatic and spectacular scenery in the country. But there is no escaping the rain. One online wit posted that it had only rained twice last summer – once for thirty-five days and once for sixty-four days.

And on the west coast they have a foolproof way of predicting the weather. They say that if you look out to the west and you can see the Isle of Arran, then it's going to rain. If you can't see it, then it's already raining.

'It's fine Scottish weather we're having. The rain is falling straight down and kind of to the side like.'
SIR WILLIAM WALLACE IN *BRAVEHEART* (1995)

34

THE COLD EAST

The east coast of Scotland tends to be a good deal colder than the west, especially when there's a wind blowing from the north-east that whips across the North Sea and hits the beaches with a coldness that can take your breath away. The east coast also has less rain than the west because, by the time the prevailing weather systems have washed the streets of Glasgow and turned the Highland mountain tops white with snow, there's not that much left to dampen spirits in the east.

The east coast does, however, have its own weather-related peculiarities, such as the haar mist that drifts in off the sea and rolls up the rivers like a gas attack. At its coldest, when it retreats back out to sea or otherwise dissipates, a haar will leave leafless winter trees frozen and sparkling, and frost standing up on the pavements like white grass.

Like the rest of Scotland, of course, if you don't like the weather you're having, follow local advice and wait five minutes for something different to come along!

'The Scottish sun, shocked by having its usual cloudy underpinnings stripped away, shone feverishly, embarrassed by its nakedness.'

STUART HADDON

SCOTLAND'S MAELSTROM

The Gulf of Corryvreckan lies between the islands of Jura and Scarba off Scotland's west coast. It is here that a strange phenomenon occurs at certain times of the tide. The raging waters of the Atlantic surging in, combined with the shape of the seabed, creates the Corryvreckan Whirlpool, said to be the world's third largest whirlpool. Standing waves can reach heights of up to 15 feet (4.6 metres) with currents racing along at up to 10 mph (16 km/h). That can be a very dangerous thing. A woman once drowned in a Dundee cake mixture when she was pulled in by a strong currant.

It is at Corryvreckan that, according to legend, the evil witch of winter washes her plaid, churning the water until her cloth is white and can be laid across the land as snow. There's somebody that you wouldn't want to be stuck behind in the queue at the dry cleaner's.

Another story goes that a brave prince from Scandinavia came to court the beautiful daughter of the Lord of the Isles and the lord told him that he could only have his daughter if he could keep his boat out on Corryvreckan for three days. The prince accepted the challenge, attempting to hold his boat steady using a rope wound with hemp, a rope wound with wool and a rope wound with the hair of a fair maiden, who must surely have been known from then on as a fairly bald maiden. Sadly, the Corryvreckan Whirlpool got the better of the prince, drawing him down into the depths and neither he nor his boat were ever seen again.

'And the earth was formless and there was darkness and God looked at the darkness and said, "There ye are – another wet night in Govan."'

THE REVEREND I. M. JOLLY
(AKA RIKKI FULTON)

SCOTCH MIST

Just as the wonderful Billy Connolly described Scotland as having only the two seasons, there are also two versions of what 'Scotch Mist' means. One is the freezing cold, heavily damp, penetrating mist that occurs, especially in mountain valleys. It's not quite rain, but it might as well be because it leaves you as wet as a weekend in Ullapool.

The second meaning of Scotch Mist is, apparently, something that doesn't really exist. It is something that is very hard to find, something that you think you should be able to go looking for and easily find, but turns out always to be just out of sight.

How the second version came to be is a mystery, because there is nothing hard to find about the very real, bone-chillingly damp Scotch Mist that is an infamous constituent of Scotland's weather. There was an online comment in Scotland recently about the charity fund-raising activity the Ice Bucket Challenge, 'or, as we call it, going outside'!

'There is no sunlight in the poetry of exile. There is only mist, wind, rain, the cry of the curlew and the slow clouds above damp moorland. That is the real Scotland; that is the Scotland whose memory rings the withers of the far-from-home; and, in some way that is mysterious, that is the Scotland that even a stranger learns to love.'

H. V. MORTON

SNAW, SNEESL AND FLINDRIKIN

It is often said that the native people who inhabit the Arctic regions of Siberia, Alaska, Canada and Greenland have at least fifty words for snow. Now it has been revealed by a research team from Glasgow University that the native people who inhabit Stirling, Arbroath, Cumnock and Poundland have at least 421 words for snow including 'snaw', 'sneesl' (to begin to snow) and 'flindrikin' (a slight snow shower). Why?

Scotland actually doesn't get much snow – not compared with the aforementioned Inuit territories, anyway. It snows in the Highlands more than anywhere else where, in the mountains, there may be up to around 100 days in the year when it might snow to a greater or lesser degree. Some parts of Scotland can go through the whole winter without ever seeing snow. It can get cold, especially in the mountains where the lowest recorded temperatures have been about –27°C (–16.6°F), but that was exceptional. The average winter temperature low is only 0°C (32°F). Scotland, you see, particularly on the west coast, is protected by the Gulf Stream. The warm air flow that accompanies the current that flows from the Gulf of Mexico all the way across the Atlantic to the Arctic keeps Scotland cosy.

Should, as environmentalists are warning, the ice cap at the North Pole (one of the factors that drives the Gulf Stream) recede, resulting in the Gulf Stream shutting down, it would mean a significant change in the weather not only in Scotland but in the whole of the UK. Edinburgh and Glasgow are on the same latitude as Moscow and Copenhagen in the east and Goose Bay in Canada to the west – where the average *high* temperature in the depths of winter is –12°C (10.4°F).

If Scotland had a climate like Goose Bay, we would need all of our 421 words for snow and no doubt use a lot of words that sound awfully like flindrikin.

'I do miss Glasgow but Malibu is home now. I love it here and when I do go back to Scotland it takes me a bit of time to acclimatize. I am a spoilt so-and-so. I live in the mountains of Malibu in the most gorgeous house and I phone my mum every day and tell her that I have got bad news – that it is only seventy degrees here.'

TOMMY FLANAGAN

SLIPPING AND SLIDING

A Dundee woman once shocked her young grandson (me) when she demonstrated what happened to people who laughed at her. Pavements in east-coast towns can become very slippery when rain or mist from the previous day has frozen overnight. In the bright sunshine of a cold early morning, that ice can be very difficult to spot, as this poor woman found to her cost when she slipped and fell, breaking her wrist.

When her grandson (still me) next saw her, she had a plaster cast, or stookie, on her arm and her husband had a small cut on his head. The grandson (that would be me) asked if he had slipped on ice as well.

'No,' said the woman. 'He was laughing so much about me falling over, I gied him a dunt wi my stookie!'

And, by way of demonstration, she clonked him on the head with said stookie. Then they both fell about laughing at the shocked look on the grandson's (my) face. They had been winding me up.

Falling on the pavement, however, was not uncommon in Scotland. Chic Murray once recalled: 'So there I was lying in the gutter. A man stopped and asked, "What's the matter? Did you fall over?" So I said, "No. I've a bar of toffee in my back pocket and I was just trying to break it."'

'I hate all those weathermen who tell you that rain is bad weather. There's no such thing as bad weather – just the wrong clothing. So get yourself a sexy raincoat and live a little!'

BILLY CONNOLLY

THE GREAT STORM

The worst storm ever to hit Scotland happened in 1968. Scotland, as we all know, is no stranger to storms. Two weeks of wind and rain near Loch Lomond is known as the summer holiday, but in January 1968 central Scotland experienced a storm the likes of which had never been seen before.

At around 3.00 a.m. on Monday 15 January, a storm that would become known as Hurricane Low Q charged in from the Atlantic and hit Glasgow. Roofs were ripped off buildings; blocks of high-rise flats, which were then Europe's tallest, began swaying violently and were evacuated; seven ships were sunk on the Clyde; more than 300 homes were destroyed and 70,000 were damaged; Glasgow was plunged into darkness, with no electricity. Nine people were killed overnight in Glasgow and several more were to die in accidents over the coming days as weakened walls collapsed and frantic work was undertaken to effect repairs to roofs. The storm swept on to cause more havoc and devastation across Scotland's central belt, but it was Glasgow that was hit hardest.

The weather forecast the previous day had said: 'Cloudy with rain at times . . .'

'There are two seasons in Scotland – June and Winter.'

BILLY CONNOLLY

CHAPTER THREE

WHAT THE SCOTS SAY ABOUT THEMSELVES

You don't have to paint your face blue-and-white, wear a ginger 'Jimmy wig' and shout 'FREEDUMM!!' wherever you go to be Scottish. We're not really so different from everyone else; we just happen to come from the finest country on the face of the planet. Multi-millionaire industrialist Andrew Carnegie put it quite poetically (for a multi-millionaire industrialist) when he said of the Scotsman, 'Touch his head and he will bargain and argue with you to the last. Touch his heart and he falls upon your breast.'

GINGER AND LOVING IT

Scots across the nation rejoiced when a campaign to persuade the technology giant Apple to devise and release emojis of characters with ginger hair recently achieved its aim. Around 13 per cent of Scots have the ginger gene, compared to 1–2 per cent of the population of the whole world, and it is yet another trait of which Scots are justly proud. Gone are the days when redheads were taunted and bullied; now it is a cause for celebration.

Famously flame-haired Scottish actress Karen Gillan shot to fame as the Doctor's assistant in the BBC TV show *Doctor Who*, but when she moved on to appear in the Marvel movie *Guardians of the Galaxy* in 2014, she had to have her head shaved. 'I got teased for having red hair when I was younger,' said Karen, 'which is strange because I'm Scottish and there are loads of us … we should unite forces! I love my red hair. I like having hair that looks like a volcano erupting.'

Karen's hair has now all grown back, but while it was doing so she was so loath to lose her old locks that she kept the strands of shaved hair in a plastic bag.

'It was great having red hair as a kid because then I had something to blame my temper on.'

ISLA FISHER

FACING UP TO GINGER

It can sometimes transpire that even those Scots who have previously been disappointed at showing no sign of having inherited the ginger gene can suddenly begin to display joyfully ginger symptoms. Actor James McAvoy is just such an occasional ginger.

'I always have a beard between jobs,' he told one interviewer. 'I just let it grow until they pay me to shave it. People are quite surprised it's ginger. Sometimes they ask me if I dye my hair and I always say, "No way! I'm trans-ginger."'

'No, everything's in perfect working order!'

RESPONSE TO THE QUESTION
'IS ANYTHING WORN UNDER THE KILT?'

A CRUMMY FORD FIESTA

Someone had displayed a decidedly curious sense of humour when a Dundee motorist went to his car one morning in 2012 to discover that it didn't look quite the same as the Ford Fiesta he had parked in the street the previous day. The car had been extensively restyled and customized during the night by having its bonnet, windows and roof covered in slices of bread. Up to fifteen loaves had been used, with each individual slice taped into place like a

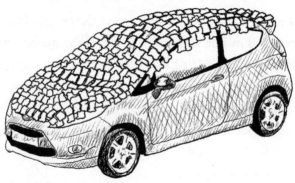

strange kind of crusty mosaic. No one was ever quite sure what sort of statement, or sandwich, the artist was trying to make . . .

'I'm half-Jewish, half-Scottish. It's hard for me to buy anything.'

DAVID DUCHOVNY

THE SCOTTISH GENE

You'd imagine that someone who has been an international singing star for most of her life, used to appearing on stage in front of thousands of people and in front of millions on TV, would be calm, confident and able to express herself openly. That, however, is not really the Scottish way. While many Scots appear gregarious and extrovert, there is also a malignant Scottish inferiority gene that can cause a huge lack of confidence. Lulu admits to not always being as bright and bubbly as her public persona.

'"I'm fine", that's what I always say,' she revealed in a recent interview. 'I'm fine. Let me tell you what my brother says FINE means . . . F***ing Incapable of Normal Expression!'

'There is some really good crack when I come back here [Scotland]. This is where I learned to swear.'

EWAN McGREGOR

SCOTS GENEROSITY

During the First World War, 'Tank Banks' toured Britain to encourage people to buy war bonds. These were real tanks, a new weapon of war that most people would never have seen before, so they attracted a lot of attention. Demonstrations of the tanks' capabilities were given and then bank clerks would sell war bonds to the spectators.

When appearing on the BBC panel show *QI*, actor David Tennant rebuffed a comment about the Scots being mean by recounting the story of the Tank Banks and pointing out that more money was raised by Tank Banks in Glasgow than in any other city in Britain. Thinking that money was actually thrown into the tank, comedian Lee Mack quipped, 'Yes, but only because they thought it was a one-armed bandit!'

For most people in Scotland, the most regular outlet for charitable donations has always been the collection plate at church, which has often suffered from traditional

Scots frugality. One minister is said to have looked at the collection plate after his sermon and seeing three pennies among the donations he immediately knew who had put them there.

'I see one of the McLeans was in today,' he said to his verger.

'Not at all,' said the verger. 'There were three of them.'

Pennies in the collection plate are not rare, but neither are banknotes, in moderation, as illustrated by the tale of two well-worn £1 and £20 Royal Bank of Scotland notes arriving together at the bank's headquarters in Edinburgh, where they were to be withdrawn from service. As they sat in a cash drawer together, awaiting their fate, the notes shared their experiences of life in circulation.

'I have been all over Scotland,' said the £20 note. 'I've been to Edinburgh Airport, nightclubs in Glasgow, a casino in Aberdeen, fine hotels in the Highlands and more swanky restaurants then I can ever remember.'

'Sounds fabulous,' said the £1 note. 'I've been in collection plates in the Church of Scotland, the Catholic Church, the Free Church of Scotland ...'

'Can I just ask ...' interrupted the £20 note, '... what's a church?'

'If you went for a job interview in a Glasgow law firm, they used to ask you what school you went to. And that was a way of finding out what religion you were.'

DENISE MINA

THE SUNDAY-SCHOOL BEAR

Such is the suspicion with which most Scots view any kind of religious practice even remotely different to their own, that an Inverness woman was more than perplexed when her daughter came home from Sunday school with a strange tale. When asked what they had been doing that morning, the little girl replied, 'We learned a new song about a cross-eyed bear called Gladly.'

Determined to find out what nonsense the Sunday-school teacher had been filling her child's head with, she phoned the church only to discover that the class had been singing the hymn 'Keep Thou My Way', which was written by an American lyricist with the unlikely name of Fanny Crosby. The penultimate line of the last verse ends with 'gladly the cross I'll bear'.

'I proved to my own satisfaction that I am madder than I think.'

CRAIG FERGUSON

RELIGION AT A PRICE

When Brodie, his favourite old Labrador died, the laird on the local estate visited the pub in town where he was fairly sure he would find the priest.

'Would you give him a nice funeral, Father?' he asked the priest.

'Out of the question,' spluttered the priest. 'Ask the minister.'

'Thank you, Father, I will,' said the laird. 'Do you think that a thousand pounds would be a decent sum to offer him for his church fund?'

'On the other hand,' said the priest, 'Brodie was a fine Catholic Labrador, was he not?'

'I'm crazy. I know I'm crazy because Desmond Tutu told me, and he's very clever. He said, "You must free yourself, be more of who you are. Be more crazy." And I'm going to.'

CRAIG FERGUSON

FOOTBALL IN PARADISE

A young Catholic priest and an equally young Protestant minister in Dundee made friends over a drink following a football match between their respective churches. They both loved the game so much that, despite their religious differences, they became firm friends. They had a long discussion about whether there was football in heaven, although neither could think of any part of the Bible that would confirm that the game was played there. Sadly, the minister died after being hit by a bus a few days later and the priest duly went to his funeral.

'If there is football in heaven,' he whispered by the graveside, 'please just give me a sign.'

That night the priest woke from a deep sleep to see the spirit of his friend standing at the foot of his bed. 'The good news,' said the minister, 'is that there is football in heaven.'

'That's wonderful,' said the priest.

'The bad news,' said the minister, 'is that your name's on the team sheet for Saturday.'

'My wife's great grandfather was killed at Custer's Last Stand. He didn't actually take part in the fighting. He was camping nearby and went over to complain about the noise.'

RONNIE CORBETT

THE BUS DRIVER'S DILEMMA

National Express takes the conduct of its drivers very seriously indeed, as it should. In 2012, the company sacked one driver in Scotland for making obscene gestures to a 'bus spotter'.

The following year the company had another problem when a driver refused to pick up children that he was supposed to be taking to school in Dundee. Instead of stopping for the kids, he sailed straight past them and, when challenged about his behaviour, he said that he didn't do so because he was a psychic. He had had a premonition that if he allowed the children on board, something absolutely terrible was going to happen. It did. He was sacked. The word around Dundee at the time was simply, 'He should have seen that coming.'

'It is one of the most hauntingly beautiful places in the world. The history is fascinating, the men are handsome and the whisky is delicious. But don't eat the macaroni pies.'

J. K. ROWLING

LAST WISH

The reading of a last will and testament is a serious affair, so there were no smiles when it came to reciting the bequests and last requests of a deceased friend in the office of a Perth solicitor. The man who had passed on had been a good and loyal husband to his house-proud wife all of his married life. He had been known to wash the windows every weekend; always to use a coaster under his cup of tea; never to put his feet on the furniture; always to put the toilet seat down when he had finished and to redecorate each room of the house in strict rotation. In short, the poorman was henpecked for decades. No one was surprised when his last wish was that his ashes should be put in an urn decorated with a thistle and a saltire, carried to his house by a kilted pall-bearer … and then scattered on the living-room carpet.

'I thought I'd rather do bad movies than bad television because you get more money for it.'

BRIAN COX

NO MEAN THREAT

There was a rumour that went around the newspaper staff and reporters in London's Fleet Street, when it was still the heart of the newspaper business in Britain, that one of the London editors had received a letter from a furious reader in Aberdeen. The editor had printed an article that included references to how famously frugal the Scots are, reinforcing the old 'mean Scotsman' stereotype. The letter warned the editor against portraying the Scots as mean, and threatened that, 'If you print any more jokes about mean Scotsmen I shall stop borrowing your newspaper.'

'But I do like Scotland. I like the miserable weather. I like the miserable people, the fatalism, the negativity, the violence that's always just below the surface. And I like the way you deal with religion. One century you're up to your lugs in it, the next you're trading the whole apparatus in for Sunday superstores. Praise the Lord and thrash the bairns. Ask and ye shall have the door shut in your face. Blessed are they that shop on the Sabbath, for they shall get the best bargains. Oh yes, this is a very fine country.'

JAMES ROBERTSON, FROM HIS NOVEL *THE TESTAMENT OF GIDEON MACK* (2006)

BEAUTIFUL NAIRN

The World's Worst Poet, William Topaz McGonagall, travelled all over Scotland during his lifetime. Some might suggest that this was because he was thrown out of more towns in the country than anyone else in order that the inhabitants could avoid being subjected to any more of his recitations. Yet no one could deny that he appreciated the glorious beauty of Scotland, even if he then mangled it in verse, as he does here in these selected verses from his poem, 'Beautiful Nairn':

All ye tourists who wish to be away
From the crowded city for a brief holiday;
The town of Nairn is worth a visit, I do confess,
And it's only about fifteen miles from Inverness.

And in the summer season it's a very popular
  bathing-place,
And the visitors from London and Edinburgh find
  solace,
As they walk along the yellow sand beach inhaling
  fresh air;
Besides, there's every accommodation for ladies and
  gentlemen there.

Then there's the ancient stronghold of the Bays of
  Lochloy,
And visitors when they see it will it heartily enjoy;
And a little further on there's the blasted heath of
  Macbeth,
And a hillock where the witches are wont to dance till
  out of breath.

And in conclusion I will say for good bathing Nairn is
  the best,
And besides its pleasant scenery is of historical interest;
And the climate gives health to many visitors while
  there,
Therefore I would recommend Nairn for balmy pure
  air.

SCHOOL WAR CRIMES

Scottish author Mason Cross was astounded when his eleven-year-old daughter challenged her teachers, accusing them of being war criminals on a simple pupil feedback form. Taking a typically Scottish combative stance, she had used the form to campaign for social justice in the classroom. In the part of the form headed, 'Things my teacher(s) can do better', she wrote:

'Not use collective punishment as it is not fair on the many people who did nothing and under the 1949 Geneva Conventions it is a war crime.'

Her father tweeted that he was 'not sure if I should ground her or buy her ice cream'.

'If Freud had worn a kilt in the prescribed Highland manner, he might have had a different attitude to genitals.'

ANTHONY BURGESS

THE PURITANICAL SCOTS

Scottish people have the reputation for being party animals, enjoying drinking and dancing and generally having a good time, but there has always been a puritanism among those with a religious conviction. Britain's first Labour Party

Prime Minister, Ramsay MacDonald, had strong Scottish views on most things, including the situation that developed shortly after he left Downing Street, when George V died and his son, Edward VIII, became King. The crisis that developed over the King's romance with divorcée Wallis Simpson, who was still married to her second husband, brought the following comment from MacDonald: 'The people of this country do not mind fornication [he had six children], but they loathe adultery.'

'Guys go to the gym and train for hours and hours to pick up something that is heavier than them. Why would you want to do that?'

ROBERT CARLYLE

A WASTED WALK

Dundee has long been known as a place where drugs of all kinds have been easily obtainable. Cannabis came in from Bangladesh along with the jute that, up to the 1970s, was spun and woven in the city's jute mills, inspiring a flourishing drugs culture in the city. But who would have thought that, in 2015, a seven-month-old border terrier called Teddy would become part of the city's drugs problem? Teddy started staggering around and behaving oddly during a walk in the park and, when taken to a vet, it was discovered that the zonked-out pup had got himself into a state by eating mushrooms growing in the grass. With some TLC from the vet and his owners, Teddy managed to shake off his trip in the park, but when the local newspaper got hold of the story, the headlines on the hoardings read: Dog Stoned On 'Magic Mushies'.

'It's SHITE being Scottish! We're the lowest of the low. The scum of the f***ing Earth! The most wretched, miserable, servile, pathetic trash that was ever shat into civilization. Some people hate the English. I don't. They're just wankers. We, on the other hand, are colonized by wankers. Can't even find a decent culture to be colonized by. We're ruled by effete assholes.'

MARK RENTON IN *TRAINSPOTTING* (1996)

CHAPTER FOUR

PECULIAR SCOTTISH FOLKLORE

Scotland is so full of strange creatures that it's a wonder there is any room at all left for the Scots. If all of the myths and legends are to be believed (and they're not) then the sea, the rivers, the lochs, the fields, the forests and the mountains are rampant with all manner of beasties that are not of this world. Here are some of the less famous stories, myths and legends to keep you on your toes.

THE GORBALS VAMPIRE

Hundreds of schoolchildren from the Gorbals area of Glasgow descended on the city's Southern Necropolis one evening in September 1954, all armed with wooden staves, knives, clubs and any other improvised weapon they could find. This was not a regular event in the city, despite Glasgow's reputation – this was different. The kids were determined to hunt down a vampire with iron teeth that had killed and eaten two young boys.

The word had spread around the local schools. The vampire hunt was on – bring something to kill it with. The police were called and found the cemetery teeming with frightened but determined children. Vampires don't mess with kids from the Gorbals! One lad who was there described how the steelworks behind the cemetery made the scene even more bizarre, saying, 'The red light and smoke would flare up and make all the gravestones leap.'

The police could not disperse the vampire hunters, even when they assured them that no boys had gone missing. The brave youngsters stuck to their guns, or rather their wooden staves, right up until it started to pour with rain. Then they all trotted off home.

THE BLOB

One intriguing story from the northern isles tells how the people of Shetland were held in fear of a fat, slimy, boneless blob of a creature that they had named the 'frittening', as anyone who saw it would be frightened to death. Well, you get what you vote for in local politics.

The creature was described as slithering around in the dead of night without any arms or legs, slumping here and there like a bag of wet wool. It left a kind of snail trail wherever it went, although some believed that it could fly, soaring through the air like a misty jellyfish.

You would want to keep your curtains closed at night if the frittening was around, as it had a nasty habit of blubbering up the garden path and peering into people's houses by pressing its single, bloodshot eye against the window!

ANNIE'S ROOM

Mary King's Close in Edinburgh was once an area of tenement houses many storeys high, but is now a vaulted enclosure of seventeenth-century streets that lie beneath the City Chambers. It is an area that was believed to be haunted even before it was built over and became a subterranean warren, but there is one area of the close that still has the power to freeze your heart – Annie's Room.

In the early 1990s, when a Japanese psychic called Aiko Gibo visited Mary King's Close with a TV crew to film part of a show about the supernatural, she was disappointed not to have found any screaming banshees or despicable poltergeists to report on. Then, as she turned to leave, she froze. Her crew didn't have a clue what was happening but Aiko walked into a small room, paused for a while and then left suddenly. She said that she had been called into the room by the spirit of a child called Annie who had died of the plague. The child was desperately upset because she was all alone and had lost her doll. Annie's cold little hand then tugged at Aiko's fingers. Aiko went straight out and bought a Barbie doll to leave in the room for Annie and, ever since, tourists visiting that part of Mary King's Close have been bringing toys to help ease the torment of poor lonesome Annie.

THE FAIRY BURIAL PLACE

Have you ever had one of those strange days when you're out, say, looking for rabbit burrows on a hillside, enjoying the fresh air and the sunshine when suddenly you come across a tomb where miniature coffins have been neatly arranged as though in some fairy ceremony? No? That's what happened to three young lads roaming around on Arthur's Seat, an ancient inactive volcano in Edinburgh, in 1836.

The boys found a spot where someone had been digging into the hillside and they moved some pieces of slate aside to find seventeen tiny wooden coffins, each just 3–4 inches (up to 10cm) long. There were strange markings on the coffin lids and inside were wooden figures that had been carefully carved and dressed in custom-made clothes. Some of the cloth had rotted away, but it was clear that a great deal of thought had gone into making the effigies.

Boys will be boys, so they used the strange things as weapons to throw at each other, but some of the coffins survived and can now be seen at the National Museum of Scotland in Edinburgh. Why the coffins were created and why they were there in a hillside tomb remains a mystery. They may have been tributes to local sailors lost at sea or part of an occult ritual or may even have been put there by those who believe in fairies. One writer described the find as a 'Fairy Burial Place'.

There are those, however, who believe that the coffins were tokens to help the troubled souls of the murdered victims of Edinburgh's infamous grave robbers, William Burke and William Hare, find peace. In 1828, Burke and Hare were convicted of sixteen murders, selling the corpses for dissection at university anatomy lectures. So was there one more unknown victim?

NEVER WALK WITHERSHINS

In seventeenth-century Kirkcudbrightshire, you had to be careful where you walked, and how. One old woman who lived alone made the error of walking withershins around a well near her home. Big mistake. Any fool knows that you don't walk withershins around a well. In case you're not any fool, it means that she walked against the direction of the sun, anti-clockwise or even backwards around the well. The locals took this as definitive evidence that she was a witch.

Having been accused of not walking deasil – that's clockwise or the reverse of anything that might be termed even remotely withershinny – around a holy well, the woman was found guilty of witchcraft and had to face her punishment. A small fine, maybe? A spot of community service, perhaps? No, she was put to death by being rolled down a hill inside a blazing barrel of tar. You have been warned!

TOAST THE GHOST

Around the beginning of the twentieth century, the eccentric Major James Grant, owner of the Glen Grant distillery in Rothes on Speyside, returned from adventures in Africa with a boy who had been found wandering lost and starving in the bush. The boy was called Biawa Makalaga, and the major and his wife took him home with them to Rothes, where he was educated at the local school and given a job as a pageboy at Glen Grant House.

Biawa became a popular character in the village, with the locals referring to him as 'Byeway'. He served in the British Army during the First World War and returned to Rothes afterwards, even playing in goal for the local football team, Rothes Victoria. He continued to work for the Grant family as a butler and ended his days on Speyside.

Legend has it that, in 1979, seven years after Biawa had died, two new stills were installed at the Glenrothes distillery, not far from Biawa's former employers' Glen Grant facility, and shortly afterwards the figure of Biawa was spotted in the still room. Following another sighting, a psychic investigator was asked to pay a visit and the man spent a while gazing at the cemetery next to the distillery before walking straight up to Biawa's grave. After some time, he returned to the distillery to inform them that Biawa's spirit was being disturbed by the alignment of the new stills. Adjustments were duly made and Biawa was never seen lurking in the still room again, although it became traditional to 'Toast the Ghost' with the produce from the distillery at every given opportunity. Well, why not?

THE SCOTTISH GIANTS

There are many stories of giants in Scotland, and not just giant breakfasts to deal with your giant hangovers. The giants tended to be quite reclusive, living in the mountains or out on the far islands, and the most solitary of all inhabited the highest mountains on the farthest islands.

There were two giant brothers who lived on the Shetland island of Unst who both fell in love with the same mermaid, which sounds a bit of a fishy tale. The mermaid wasn't sure that she would be happy with either of them, but challenged them nonetheless, as mermaids are wont to do, to chase her all the way to the North Pole. Both brothers jumped into the sea to swim after her and neither of them was ever seen again, which tells you something about how gullible and slightly dopey giants can be.

An Orkney giant named Cubbie Roo was said to be so huge that he could leap from one of Orkney's many islands to another, which makes a mystery out of why he should bother to build bridges, but build them he apparently did, the rock stacks and arches around the islands remaining as evidence of his ancient architecture. Cubbie loved playing with stones and made himself a real pain in the neck by hurling them at giants on other islands. There is a monolith on Rousay known as the 'Fingersteen' because it bears Cubbie's fingermarks from when he gripped it to throw it from Westray at another giant on Kierfea Hill. He missed, but he made a big impression.

On the mainland, the people in the north of Perthshire were terrorized by the Giant of Atholl. He would appear from his cave in the forest, steal the locals' grain, carry off their sheep or cattle – he didn't bother with chickens, they just got stuck in his teeth – and batter to death anyone who tried to stop him with one swipe of his mighty fist. One day a hunter named Dougal decided that something needed to be done about the giant and tracked him to his lair. While the giant was out plundering, Dougal saw that he had accumulated several sacks of oats, many jars of honey and some casks of whisky. Knowing that he could never best the giant in a straightforward fight, he came up with a cunning plan. He poured the oats into a hollow boulder that the giant clearly used for drinking, then mixed in the honey and whisky before scuttling back to his hiding place.

When the giant returned, he soon sniffed out the concoction in his drinking boulder, gave it a sip and then downed the lot before dozing off, whereupon Dougal darted out and bravely murdered him as he slept. Dougal was hailed as a hero not only for killing the giant but also for inventing the liqueur known as Atholl Brose.

THE CANNIBAL CLAN

The eating habits of the Scots have come in for a lot of criticism over the years and it's fairly widely acknowledged that we will eat pretty much anything except for salad or each other. There are, of course, always exceptions, one of them being Sawney Bean – and no, he wasn't famous for his love of salad.

Said to have been born the son of a ditch digger in East Lothian in the sixteenth century, Alexander 'Sawney' Bean never really took to hard work and, on meeting up with a woman, the pair fled to the south-west coast where they set up home in a cave between Girvan and Ballantrae. The 660-foot (201-metre) deep cave can be found at Bennane Head, and it is there that Bean raised his clan – eight sons, six daughters and over thirty grandchildren born of incest.

So how did this growing family survive? They were not, after all, the sort of jobseekers that potential employers would be falling over each other to sign up, even if they could find them. The members of the growing Bean family, you see, were so secretive that the locals didn't even know they were there. Yet they had to eat, so they set out at night, roaming the countryside and murdering any poor unfortunate traveller they could find. The bodies were brought back to the cave where they were cut up and devoured. Some human body parts would, from time to time, be washed ashore on other beaches, the strong currents of the Clyde having carried them far from the

Beans' cave, so their gruesome secret existence continued.

Legend has it that they murdered at least 1,000 people before they were eventually hunted down after failing to subdue a victim in one of their ambushes. He escaped and an army of 400 armed men took the Beans alive, finding human remains and rugs made of skin in their cave. The men were put to death in the painfully brutal fashion of the time – think Mel Gibson in *Braveheart* with extra bits removed – while the women and children were made to watch before being burned alive.

If you are reading this last thing at night, you should know that it is believed that some of the Beans evaded capture and are still out there. So check behind the curtains …

CHAPTER FIVE

AULD ENEMY AND AULD ALLIANCE

The rivalry between the Scots and the English is very real, but is seen nowadays as a bit of fun rather than a matter of life and death. It hasn't always been that way, which is why the 'Auld Alliance' – a treaty signed in 1295 between Scotland and France that stood for over 250 years – came to be.

ENGLISH PRIDE

A Scotsman drinking at a bar in London was moaning and grumbling about the inferiority of the English, and how loathsome they were, to the extent that the barman could take it no more.

'I am proud to be English,' he said. 'I was born a true Englishman and I will die a true Englishman.'

'Ach away, man,' said the Scot. 'Have ye no ambition?'

'We look to Scotland for all our ideas of civilization.'

VOLTAIRE

VOTE YES!

When Scotland went to the polls in 2014 to vote about the future of the nation, there had been lengthy discussion over what question would actually be posed on the ballot paper. In the end, it was decided that the paper would present the question, 'Should Scotland be an independent country?' You would be able to tick a box for 'Yes' or a box for 'No'.

When the English football team played against Switzerland in Basel during the run-up to the election (England won 2–0), a crowd of exuberant English fans in one corner of the stadium were jumping up and down and singing to the tune of 'Knees Up Mother Brown':

We're all voting YES!
We're all voting YES!
F**k off Scotland,
F**k off Scotland,
We're all voting YES!

The fact that the ballot was only open to those living in Scotland and they wouldn't have any kind of vote on the matter didn't seem to bother them.

'England have got the best fans in the world – and Scotland's fans are undoubtedly second to none …'

KEVIN KEEGAN

CELEBRATORY DAMAGE

There's a common assumption that all Scots will support any team, in any sport, anywhere, if that team is playing against England, on the basis that 'any enemy of the English is a friend of mine'. It's not entirely true, but so many Scots have come to think that way that the assumption is not exactly inaccurate, either.

When it comes to celebrating victory, however, Scots can be quite generous in their support. In the wake of England's win against Sweden in the 2018 World Cup, there were enthusiastic celebrations in the streets of London. Some fans got a bit carried away and shocked the rest of the country by climbing on top of an ambulance, dancing and singing. The ambulance came off the worse for wear and had to be taken out of service, although English football fans later launched a campaign to raise funds for the repairs. One of the internet images of the over-excited fans featured a young woman in a very short pink miniskirt, dancing on the ambulance to roars of appreciation from the crowd. She turned out to be a waitress from East Kilbride in Scotland who was paying a visit to friends in London. A true, if ill-advised, demonstration of Scottish magnanimity.

'London is the devil's drawing-room.'

TOBIAS SMOLLETT

THE CREATION OF SCOTLAND

In the beginning, when God toiled to create the Earth, he spent a great deal of time concentrating on one small northern country in particular. His friend, the angel Gabriel, was watching.

'Just a minute, Lord,' said Gabriel. 'Aren't you being a bit over-generous to that place. You've given it splendid, dramatic mountains; lush, fertile valleys; rivers full of trout and salmon; fields of barley for them to make whisky; coal, oil and gas. I think that you are spoiling these people.'

'Don't worry, Gabriel,' said God. 'Wait till you see who they're getting as neighbours.'

---

*'I was born in London and went to school inScotland
– I used to be dead tired when I got home at night.'*

NORMAN WISDOM

A REWARDING EXPERIENCE

Hiking through the Highlands, an English tourist became so hopelessly lost in a thick hill fog that he could barely tell up from down and had no idea how to find his way off the mountain. Suddenly, a Highlander appeared out of the mist, wearing heavy tweeds and carrying a stout walking stave.

'Thank goodness you've found me,' said the tourist. 'I've been wandering around for two days and I'm totally lost.'

'Would there be a reward out for ye?' asked the Highlander, leaning on his stave.

'I shouldn't think so,' said the tourist.

'Then you're still lost,' said the Highlander, and disappeared off into the mist again.

---

*'It is tremendously good fun winding up the Scots.
It is terribly easy, particularly Scottish politicians.
They can take things far too seriously.'*

JEREMY PAXMAN

SCOTLAND'S 'CHIEF EXPORTS'

There were complaints to the BBC in 2013 when the topic on the TV comedy panel show *Have I Got News For You* turned to the Scottish Independence Referendum. Guest host and quizmaster on the show for that episode was actor Ray Winstone of *Scum* and *Sexy Beast*. The discussion turned to Scotland's finances and Winstone said, 'To be fair the Scottish economy has its strengths – its chief exports being oil, whisky, tartan and tramps.' He followed that up by asking the studio audience's opinion about whether 'we should just tell the Scots to bugger off'.

'The noblest prospect which a Scotchman ever sees is the high road that leads him to England.'

SAMUEL JOHNSON

THE WORLD'S MOST BEAUTIFUL COUNTRY

An English tourist stopped at a bar near Loch Ness where the barman, hearing the English accent, proudly welcomed the tourist to 'the world's most beautiful country'.

'You think so?' said the tourist. 'Take away those pretty lochs and towering mountains and what have you really got?'

The barman smiled as he placed a drink in front of his customer and said, 'England.'

'Have you ever tried to use Scottish money in England? It's hilarious. They look at you like you've just tried to pay for your shopping with a dead baby.'

MICHAEL MCINTYRE

JUST OFFAL

Most Scots are welcomed into English communities and integrate with the locals, making friends and building relationships just as people do all over the world. It is seldom that Scots come across prejudice or are harassed when they choose to move south. Unfortunately, one woman and her family living in Rochdale, Greater Manchester, became the target for a campaign of spite. Christine McKinnon had moved to England from Glasgow thirty-four years before she and her children were picked on in Rochdale, suffering taunts and verbal abuse. It was upsetting, but something that she and her family coped with.

The harassment took a bizarre turn when she

returned home from a trip to Dublin to find that her front window had been smashed. Lying in her living room amid a scattering of broken glass was … a haggis.

'Scottish people drink spasmodically and intensely, for the sake of a momentary but complete release, whereas the English like to bathe and paddle about bucolically in a mild puddle of beer.'

EDWIN MUIR

THE NAME GAME

There is a Scottish pub in Paris called the Auld Alliance where there are thistles etched into the window glass and they have Scottish 80/- ale from the Caledonian Brewery in Edinburgh on tap.

In order to extend the hand of friendship, a Frenchman and a Scotsman took an Englishman into the Auld Alliance to buy him a pint. They chatted about home, their families and their children.

'My son was born on St Andrew's Day,' said the Scotsman, 'so we called him Andrew.'

'That is such a coincidence,' said the Frenchman. 'My daughter was born on Valentine's Day, so we called her Valentine.'

'That's really quite remarkable,' said the Englishman. 'We did exactly the same with our son Pancake.'

'I'm not saying my act died in the Glasgow Empire, but an undertaker in the audience threw a tape measure at me, and some embalming fluid.'

LES DAWSON

THE VOTING DILEMMA

The Scottish Independence Referendum spawned a great deal of debate on all sorts of topics, from whether there would have to be a border between Scotland and England to the defence of the nation and the economy. There was also a huge debate about who should be allowed to vote. Youngsters of sixteen were allowed to cast a vote, but Scots who were not resident in Scotland had no vote. Nor did the population of the rest of the United Kingdom and many English people complained that they should be allowed to have a say in the decision as it was something that would have a huge effect on them. Comedian Kevin Bridges agreed. 'I think we should have an English vote first and let England make the first move,' he said. 'If they want us to leave, then we'll stay.'

'It's never difficult to distinguish between a Scotsman with a grievance and a ray of sunshine.'

P. G. WODEHOUSE

THE FAIRY GLEN

A Frenchman, a Scotsman and an Englishman were walking through the Highlands when they crested a mountain ridge to see a most beautiful glen stretching out before them, shimmering and sparkling in the sunlight when there had been no sunshine before. Purple heather glowed with a strange hue and the sweetest scents filled the air. The three stopped and marvelled at the glorious view, but could not find the glen on their map.

'Ye'll no' see this place on yer silly map,' came a voice, and they turned to see a beautiful fairy dressed in black, scowling at them. 'This is the domain of the fairy folk,' she said, 'and if ye enter ye can have whatever yer heart desires.'

All three agreed that this seemed like a good idea and asked which path they should follow down into the glen.

'There's nae path,' said the fairy. 'Ye must jump off this cliff. It's the only way. If ye survive ye may achieve yer heart's desire.'

The three looked over the cliff at the sheer drop. The fall would surely kill them. Just then another beautiful fairy appeared, this one dressed in white.

'Be brave,' she said. 'You will survive. Shout out what you would most like to land in and a pool of it will appear just before you reach the bottom.'

The Frenchman was first to go, shouting as he jumped, 'Cognaaaaaaac!' He splashed safely into a pool of the finest Cognac.

The Scotsman went next, shouting as he jumped, 'Whiskyyyyyyyyyy!' He splashed safely into a pool of excellent single malt.

The Englishman went last, shouting as he jumped, 'Oh, shiiiiiiiiiiiiiiiit!'

CHAPTER SIX

MADE IN SCOTLAND

Nobody can deny that Scotland punches well above its weight when it comes to producing bright ideas, incredible inventions and brainy types who go on to become world-renowned doctors, surgeons, scientists, engineers, designers and general geniuses. Here, then, is a list of a few things for which the world owes Scotland its gratitude. You might think that some of them have only tenuous connections to Scotland, but anything that has even a remote link will be claimed by the Scots as their own, whether it be the toilet or the tractor beam …

A

Adhesive postage stamp: invented by James Chalmers from Arbroath.

B

Bicycle: the pedal bicycle was invented by Kirkpatrick Macmillan from Keir in Dumfries and Galloway.

Bond: James Bond was created by author Ian Fleming, who was the grandson of Robert Fleming from Dundee, a merchant banker. Bond is the son of Andrew Bond from Glencoe and was famously played by Sean Connery, so you can't get much more Scottish than that.

C

Cash machines: the first automated cash machine was developed by John Shepherd-Barron, whose father was Scottish, while James Goodfellow from Paisley patented Personal Identification Number technology used in a different type of cash machine.

Cordite: the smokeless (compared with gunpowder) explosive used in shells was developed by chemist and physicist Sir James Dewar from Kincardine.

D

Dolly the sheep: the world's first cloned mammal was the work of scientists Ian Wilmut and Keith Campbell. Campbell's father was Scottish and the work was done at the Roslin Institute, which is part of Edinburgh University, so Dolly was Scottish.

'Of all the small nations of this earth, perhaps only the ancient Greeks surpass the Scots in their contribution to mankind'.

WINSTON CHURCHILL

E

Electric toaster: invented by Alan MacMasters from Edinburgh.

Electromagnetic radiation: the theory of electromagnetic radiation was devised by James Clerk Maxwell from Edinburgh.

F

Films that should have been made in Scotland:
Aberlady and the Tramp
Brechin Counter
Dumb and Dumbarton
Every Which Way But Lewis

Father of the Bridie
Forfar from the Madding Crowd
Full Methil Jacket

Flush toilet: often incorrectly credited to Englishman Thomas Crapper, the flush toilet with S-bend to retain water and banish smells was invented by Alexander Cumming from Edinburgh.

H

Hammer: the steam hammer was invented by James Nasmyth from Edinburgh.

Hypnotism: James Braid from Kinross was a surgeon who pioneered hypnotism and hypnotherapy.

I

Irn-Bru: 'Made in Scotland from girders' was how drinks company A. G. Barr advertised Scotland's other national drink. The bestselling soft drink in Scotland is not made from girders, but it does actually contain iron. It is exported all over the world and made under licence in Russia. Worldwide, Barr sells around twenty cans of Irn-Bru every second.

J

John Bull: though John Bull was perhaps typically English, his character was devised by Dr John Arbuthnot from Kincardineshire in 1712.

L

Lamp signalling: ship-to-ship signals using lamps were devised by Vice-Admiral Philip Howard Colomb from Knockbrex in Dumfries and Galloway.

Logarithms: invented by John Napier from Edinburgh.

Long John Silver: the character from *Treasure Island* was created by author Robert Louis Stevenson from Edinburgh.

M

McGonagall: the Worst Poet in the World, William McGonagall, claimed to have been born in Edinburgh in 1825 or possibly 1830, he was never quite sure – well, he was very young at the time. He may also have been confused over his birthplace and was probably actually Irish, like his parents. The place and precise year of his birth matter little now, however, as he has been claimed as a son of Dundee. Here's a snippet of what he had to say about the collapse of the Tay Bridge:

> **The Tay Bridge Disaster**
> *Beautiful Railway Bridge of the Silv'ry Tay!*
> *Alas! I am very sorry to say*
> *That ninety lives have been taken away*
> *On the last Sabbath day of 1879,*
> *Which will be remember'd for a very long time.*

Menai Suspension Bridge: designed by Thomas Telford from Eskdale, Dumfriesshire.

Movie camera: developed by Scottish inventor William Kennedy-Laurie Dickson while working for Thomas Edison.

N

Nucleus: the nucleus in living cells was first identified by Robert Brown from Montrose.

O

Oil refinery: James Young from Glasgow first refined paraffin and other oils from coal and crude oil.

Overhead cam engine: devised by the founder of the Buick car company, David Dunbar Buick, from Arbroath.

P

Penicillin: discovered in 1928 by Sir Alexander Fleming from Darvel in Ayrshire.

Peter Pan: created by J. M. Barrie from Kirriemuir in Angus.

Pneumatic tyres: invented by Robert William Thomson from Stonehaven in Aberdeenshire and John Boyd Dunlop from Dreghorn in Ayrshire.

Propeller: the first practical screw propeller for a ship was invented by Robert Wilson, a fisherman's son from Dunbar.

R

Radar: partly developed by Sir Robert Watson-Watt from Brechin, so we'll have that.

S

Sherlock Holmes: created by Sir Arthur Conan Doyle from Edinburgh.

Steam engine: James Watt from Greenock developed and improved the steam engine to the extent that it galvanized the industrial revolution.

T

Telephone: invented by Sir Alexander Graham Bell from Edinburgh.

Television: invented by John Logie Baird from Helensburgh.

Threshing machine: the forerunner of the combine harvester was invented by Andrew Meikle from East Lothian.

Tractor beam: not just something you see on *Star Trek*, the tractor beam actually exists and was developed at St Andrews University.

U

Ultrasound: developed for medical diagnosis by Scottish physician Ian Donald.

V

Vacuum flasks: invented by Sir James Dewar from Kincardine.

W

Waterproof fabric: invented by Charles Macintosh from Glasgow.

Before   After

Wave power: producing electricity from waves was devised by Stephen Salter, a South African, who was Professor of Engineering at Edinburgh University, so wave power is ours.

And finally, what about the *Encyclopaedia Britannica*? First published in Edinburgh in 1768, we claim it for Scotland. Oh, and everything in it …

CHAPTER SEVEN

MR SPEAKER!

Politics in Scotland is as varied and reactionary as it is anywhere else in the UK, with the thistle-prickly issue of independence adding an extra dash of colour, especially in recent years.

WORKING IN HARMONY

We are all used to Donald Trump's outrageous social media gaffes and political blunders, so maybe he should ask some advice from Scottish politicians about how to come across in tweets as friendly, sensible, funny and … normal.

When Andy Murray was playing Czech Tomáš Berdych in the semi-final of the Australian Open in January 2015, Ruth Davidson, leader of the Scottish Conservative Party, tweeted about a dilemma she was having just after 8 a.m.:

'Hmmm … FMQ [First Minister's Questions] prep vs tennis . . .'

Scottish First Minister, SNP leader Nicola Sturgeon, responded with: 'I'm sure we could come to some arrangement.'

Ruth Davidson replied: 'OK, I'll bring the snacks – let's use your office. Kez, you in?'

Kezia Dugdale, then Deputy Leader of the Scottish Labour Party, answered: 'Yes, there in a minute, looking for the Pimms.'

A brilliant example of cross-party political co-operation to achieve a mutually beneficial result. Murray beat Berdych but then lost to Novak Djokovic in the final.

> *'Our Scottish theory ... is that every country has*
> *need of Scotchmen, but that Scotland has no need of*
> *the citizens of any other country.'*
>
> ARTHUR BALFOUR

THE GREAT REFERENDUM

When the Scots were in the long run-up to the 2014 Independence Referendum, the Scottish National Party was rampant, inspiring a patriotic fervour that infected the entire nation, whether you were for or against independence. Such was the passion and commitment of the SNP that they seemed to fear nothing. They were convinced that Scotland was on the brink of becoming an independent nation and when Britain's three leading politicians (referred to as 'the three amigos'), Labour leader Ed Miliband, Liberal leader and Deputy Prime Minister Nick Clegg and Tory leader Prime Minister David Cameron announced that they were heading north to persuade the Scottish people to remain part of the UK, the SNP showed no fear. SNP Scottish First Minister Alex Salmond displayed a typically Scottish combination of bravado and frugality. 'If I thought they were coming by bus,' he said, 'I'd send the bus fare.'

> *'The single most important two things we can do ...'*
>
> TONY BLAIR

HER MAJESTY SPEAKS OUT

The 2014 Independence Referendum clearly caused the Queen great concern. Her mother, after all, was Scottish and the Queen spends her summer break at Balmoral Castle in Aberdeenshire. During her remarkably long reign, however, the Queen has remained steadfastly neutral on political matters, as it is the duty of the monarch to stand aside from politics, at least in public. It was, therefore, headline news when a well-wisher in the crowd waiting to greet Her Majesty as she left Crathie Kirk after a Sunday service joked about not mentioning the referendum and received the following response: 'Well, I hope people will think very carefully about the future.'

The Queen's comment was carefully worded to express her concern without appearing to take sides. When one local was asked about Her Majesty's remarks, he was rather more direct. 'My opinion is I cannae trust Salmond,' he said. 'He's got a head like a haggis and nae reason penetrates it.'

'*David Beckham sent the people of Scotland an open letter. An open letter … because he couldn't work out how to get it into an envelope.*'

FRANKIE BOYLE

SAY IT LIKE IT SOUNDS …

Scottish novelist M. C. Beaton, who created the Hamish Macbeth and Agatha Raisin characters, gave a speech at a writers' conference just before the 2014 Scottish Independence Referendum. She told a story about how the then Scottish First Minister, Alex Salmond, had a telephone conversation with the Queen.

'Your Majesty,' said Mr Salmond. 'After the vote, if Scotland is a kingdom, will I be a king?'

'No, Mr Salmond,' said the Queen. 'Scotland will not be a kingdom, so you won't be king.'

'So, Your Majesty,' said Mr Salmond. 'After the vote, if Scotland is a principality, will I be a prince?'

'No, Mr Salmond,' said the Queen. 'Scotland will not be a principality, so you won't be a prince. But Scotland *will* be a country …'

'For a leader who can stand in the proud tradition of William Wallace and Andy Murray, won't you consider the return of Scotland's prodigal son … Groundskeeper Willie? I've lived in America most of my life, so I've seen first-hand how not to run a country.'

GROUNDSKEEPER WILLIE
FROM *THE SIMPSONS*

USE THE FORCE ...

At public meetings, Members of Parliament are used to having to deal with those who may not entirely agree with their point of view. A particularly vocal dissenter can even be used to a speaker's advantage in a lively debate, but sometimes MPs get more than they bargain for. A group of English Labour MPs visited Glasgow prior to the Scottish Independence Referendum in an effort to persuade people to vote to stay part of the UK. They had to contend with a heckler who called out, 'Bow down, people of Glasgow! Bow down to your imperial masters! Be grateful! They've travelled all this way! Don't worry, they'll put it on expenses! Bow down!' This might not have been so hard to deal with had the heckler not been riding around in a rickshaw with a massive sound system blasting out Darth Vader's theme from *Star Wars*.

IT'S LEGAL TENDER!

There is a cry often heard in English stores when visiting Scots try to use Scottish banknotes and the shop assistant gives them a funny look – 'It's legal tender!'. Staff in most big stores in England are aware of the existence of Scottish banknotes, even though they may not come across them very often, but, despite the protestations of the Scots, the notes are not actually legal tender anywhere in the UK,

including Scotland. They are, in fact, 'promissory notes' and the banks that issue them – Clydesdale Bank, Bank of Scotland and Royal Bank of Scotland – are required to hold Bank of England notes or gold to the equivalent amount to cover the value of the notes issued.

In Scotland, of course, we are fiercely proud of having our own money and, although they are now as rare as wild haggis, there are even still a few £1 notes in circulation in Scotland. The Scots did not really take to the £1 coin and when the latest version was launched in March 2017 it inspired a joke that was voted most popular at the 2017 Edinburgh Fringe Festival. Comedian Ken Cheng said, 'I'm not a fan of the new pound coin, but then again, I hate all change.'

'Bonnie Prince Charlie was the only man ever named after three sheepdogs.'

BILLY CONNOLLY

TWIT OR TWEET?

Although former Prime Minister David Cameron was born and raised in England, he has a distinctly Scottish name, his father having been born in Aberdeenshire. Cameron himself, referencing his mother's side of the family, once said, 'I'm a real mixture of Scottish, Welsh and English,' thus giving himself the best chance to curry favour in all three nations. Of course, that also gave the Scots the opportunity to claim him as one of our own when it suits us or to reject him as a southerner whenever we like. So, when he says something daft enough to go in this book, he's Scottish.

We certainly saw him as one of ours when he appeared on Absolute Radio as Leader of the Opposition in 2009. Cameron was interviewed by Christian O'Connell on his breakfast show, broadcast nationwide, and the DJ asked him about using modern technology – was he on Twitter, for example?

'No, I'm not on Twitter,' said Cameron. 'The thing is that ... Politicians do have to think about what we say and the trouble with Twitter and the ... instantness of it ... is that too many twits might make a twat.'

Cameron's press office later issued an apology and he was certainly forgiven for getting 'twit' mixed up with 'tweet'.

'So after a lovely family Xmas day, this 80s
teen is off to bed feeling a bit sad, but listening to
this masterpiece [George Michael – "I Can't
Make You Love Me"].'

TWEET FROM SCOTTISH FIRST MINISTER,
NICOLA STURGEON

SATAN – MP FOR DUNDEE EAST

Dundee became infamous for political corruption in the 1970s, with one leading councillor serving a jail sentence for accepting bribes related to the awarding of building contracts. Standing in local elections, given the reputation of politicians in the city, was not something to be entered into lightly. The people of Dundee came to agree wholeheartedly with Billy Connolly, who said, 'The desire to be a politician should be enough to ban you from ever becoming one.'

During one election campaign, a worthy candidate was being constantly heckled by a woman in the crowd as he gave a public address. He finally paused when the woman yelled at him, 'I'd vote for the Devil before I'd vote for the likes of you!'

'That may be,' said the candidate, 'but your father's not standing, is he?'

> *'It seemed like after the 80s and 90s there came a sort of weird time in politics, where something like* Spitting Image *was no longer feasible because politicians weren't the big personalities that they once were. But now it seems like we're coming out of that, I mean we've got Boris Johnson, and Trump overseas, and Jeremy Corbyn.'*

ARMANDO IANNUCCI

BEMUSING BLAIRISMS

Unlike Tory Prime Minister David Cameron, Labour Prime Minister Tony Blair never played down his Scottish roots and the people of Scotland loved him for that. They also loved him for breathing new life into the moribund Labour Party but, like the rest of the country, the Scots fell out of love with him when he allowed himself to be seen as a warmongering sidekick to America's President George W. Bush. Well, we all make mistakes and it's a little surprising that Blair, who was such a good orator, made some of his when he became tangled up in his own words.

Who can forget Prime Minister Blair's words when he arrived for talks in Belfast that would lead to the Good Friday Agreement in 1998. 'A day like today is not a day for sound bites,' he said, 'but I feel the hand of history upon our shoulder . . .'

And no journalist could ever ask the Prime Minister about what might happen in days, weeks or months to come without a smile on his or her face after Blair declared, 'I don't make predictions. I never have and I never will.'

Then, when Prime Minister Blair visited Glasgow, he found himself in the midst of the usual throng of elbow-jostling news crews and photographers. He is reported to have muttered to his driver, standing at his shoulder, 'Have you ever seen such a bunch of unreconstructed w****rs?' To his horror he then realized that his driver was at his other shoulder and that the man to whom he had addressed his comment was, in fact, one of the yet-to-be-reconstructed journalists.

'There's something inherently comic about the fact that politicians make things worse by worrying too much about something.'

ARMANDO IANNUCCI

DOING TIME

Gordon Brown told how, when he was Prime Minister, he was with Nelson Mandela at a charity concert and when they went to meet the singers after the show, one of the first people who came up to talk to them was Amy Winehouse. She said to Mandela, 'Mr Mandela, my husband and you have a lot in common.' 'Really?' said Mandela. 'Yes,' said Winehouse. 'You've both spent a long time in prison.'

YOU'RE HAVING A LAUGH

Two Scotsmen were leaving the House of Lords in 2009 following the Queen's Speech. One was Prime Minister Gordon Brown and the other was Leader of the Opposition David Cameron – his father was Scottish, remember. Journalists and other observers were amazed to see Gordon Brown laughing, which is not usual when the PM and his greatest rival are obliged to rub shoulders in this way. When questioned about why the PM was laughing, one Downing Street insider suggested that the PM must have been making an extra effort not to look morose, something of which he was often accused, because there was no way that David Cameron would ever have said anything amusing.

'Do you think George Bush actually knows who Gordon Brown is? He probably just thinks Tony Blair's put on weight and had a mild stroke.'

FRANKIE BOYLE

JUNGLE KEZ

MSP (Member of the Scottish Parliament) Kezia Dugdale was Leader of the Scottish Labour Party for two years until her resignation in August 2017. Later that year she appeared in the reality TV show *I'm a Celebrity … Get Me*

Out of Here! in the jungle in Australia, where contestants face a torture of trials involving snakes, rats, insects and eating parts of animals that most starving hyenas would rather not touch. In Scotland, Kezia was predicted to do well simply because, having been involved in Labour Party meetings for most of her adult life, she was used to being trapped in an enclosed space with a shower of cockroaches.

'Laurel and f***ing Hardy! Glad you could join us. Did you manage to get that piano up the stairs OK?'

PETER CAPALDI AS PM'S ADVISER
MALCOLM TUCKER IN *THE THICK OF IT*

Q. How many MSPs does it take to change a light bulb?
A. Five. One to change the bulb and the other four to tell everyone how much brighter it would be if only Scotland were an independent nation.

'I was heckled once in Glasgow. I took that as a positively warm reception. If they love you there, they let you live.'

CHARLES KENNEDY

DOWNFALL OF THE GREATEST BRITON

In a 2002 poll to find the person whom the great British public deemed the 'Greatest Briton', British bulldog Sir Winston Churchill came top, although he hasn't always been seen as the greatest by the people of Scotland.

He became MP for Dundee in 1908, the people of the city taking to the young (he was then thirty-three), charismatic Boer War hero. He was 'parachuted' into Dundee as a rising star of the Liberal Party and the city was a Liberal safe seat at the time. Churchill could never have been said to be in love with the city, though, once writing to his wife, Clemmie, 'This city will kill me. Halfway through my kipper this morning an enormous maggot crawled out and flashed his teeth at me … Such are the penalties which great men pay in the service of their country.'

Dundee voters were far from happy about Churchill's infrequent visits, feeling neglected as the great man concentrated on his own career. He was Home Secretary for the first few months of the 'Great Unrest' of 1910–1914, and caused great concern among the workers in Dundee when he sent troops to control strikes in militant industrial areas. Workers were shot dead in Liverpool and in Wales. Also, following the First World War, Churchill was responsible for deploying the hated 'Black and Tan' paramilitary force in Ireland during the Irish War of

Independence, a move that did not go down well with Dundee's strong Irish population.

Then, during the general election of 1922, Churchill was unable to campaign effectively in Dundee as he was recovering from an appendectomy, following a bout of appendicitis. He could not walk any distance and hired men to carry him in a seat so that he could address a public gathering. While there, a Dundonian in the crowd asked one of the men how much he was being paid.

'A pound,' came the reply.

'I'll gie ye twa tae drop him!' was the response.

Churchill later reflected on his defeat, commenting that he left Dundee 'without an office, without a seat, without a party and without an appendix'.

'Three million pounds for the funeral of Margaret Thatcher? For three million pounds you could give everyone in Scotland a shovel and we'd dig a hole so deep we could hand her over to Satan in person.'

FRANKIE BOYLE

PUBLIC SERVANT BOB SERVANT

It was a sad day when Broughty Ferry's MP was brutally decapitated in a car crash, but not for cheeseburger tycoon Bob Servant. For Bob, it was a day of opportunity and he launched himself into the murky world of local politics.

A straight talker, there was much that other political personalities could learn from Mr Servant, who wrote in his autobiography that, 'If you're a big fish and you want to write a book, then the autobiography pond is the only place worth swimming. Jesus kicked it all off with the Bible and every star name since has had a crack.'

Bob, in fact, was the creation of writer Neil Forsyth and was played by Brian Cox in two BBC TV comedy series.

'I was the future once.'

DAVID CAMERON

CHAPTER EIGHT

DEEP-FRIED HAGGIS

Everyone has heard how bad the food is in Scotland, and everyone has heard wrong. There is loads of good stuff to eat in Scotland. We have the finest game, the freshest fish, the most wonderful fruit and the best local produce anywhere in the world, but it has to be said that, in the past, we have been guilty of leaving all that sort of stuff to the tourists …

FISHY TALE

It was a sad day in St Andrews when Big Mac went missing. No, it wasn't a large person's raincoat, neither was it a local worthy or a golfer on the Old Course. Big Mac was the mascot of St Andrews Aquarium – a six-foot-tall silver mackerel. John Mace, the aquarium's managing director, offered a 'no questions asked' amnesty for the return of the fish statue, commenting that, 'He's quite heavy and it would have taken two or three people to lift him.'

Those who worked at the aquarium hoped that the theft was a simple student prank and that Big Mac would be safely returned as they were missing him. As Mr Mace put it, 'Staff are gutted ...'

'For what we are about to eat, may the Lord make us truly not vomit.'

GORDON RAMSAY IN *HELL'S KITCHEN*

DUNDEE CAKE

Fruit cake has always been popular in Scotland and the fruit farms of Angus provide an abundance of raspberries, blackberries, strawberries and tayberries. Close proximity to Dundee gave the city one of its famous 'Three Js' – Jute, Jam and Journalism – the fruit farms obviously providing the raw product for jam.

Dundee cake has been made in the city and the east coast area since the nineteenth century, although legend has it that it can trace its history back further than that. It is said that Mary, Queen of Scots, who was beheaded on the orders of Queen Elizabeth I in 1587, did not like cherries in her fruit cake and the Dundee cake recipe was originally prepared for her, using almonds along with the other fruit instead of cherries and a decoration of almonds on top. Apparently she quite liked it, but didn't lose her head over it.

'Who discovered we could get milk from cows and what did he think he was doing at the time?'

BILLY CONNOLLY

THE GLASGOW OYSTER

Lebowskis pub/restaurant in Glasgow, famous for producing towering burgers that stand so tall a hippo would have trouble getting his gums round them, have produced a fabulous dish that they have named the 'Glasgow Oyster'. Between the two halves of a bun they have packed two thick and juicy beefburgers, melted mature Cheddar, a bit of salad on top and – right in the middle – a Scotch pie, all dribbling with beef-dripping gravy. The droolingly fabulous tower of calories is enough to ensure that even a teenager with the famous Scottish 'hollow legs' is not going to leave the premises hungry and stop off for chips 'n' sauce on the way home.

'It was a pretty posh place. They were so used to fur coats that two bears strolled in and ordered lunch and nobody even noticed.'

CHIC MURRAY

'The typical Scot has bad teeth, a good chance of cancer, a liver under severe stress and a heart attack pending. He smokes like a chimney, drinks like a fish, and regularly makes an exhibition of himself. Apart from that he's fine.'

ALAN BOLD

THE HUMBLE SCOTCH PIE

Pies are not, of course, unique to Scotland. Even the mutton pies so beloved of the Scots are actually produced elsewhere, so to make sure that there is no confusion when it comes to purchasing this culinary delight, ours are called Scotch pies.

We don't much like using the word Scotch nowadays. In times gone by Scotsmen (and women) were commonly referred to as Scotchmen, but in modern parlance the term is reserved for pies, eggs and whisky. In short, it's too good a word to waste on people!

Also known as the football pie (fitba' peh) because it is every football fan's favourite, the Scotch pie is traditionally filled with minced mutton heavily seasoned with pepper in a hot water crust pastry. Every baker in Scotland sells Scotch pies and the precise recipe for the filling and the pastry will vary. The correct method of eating a pie is not sedately with a fork and knife, but with your bare hands as you're walking along or watching the match. You pick it up, shove it in your mouth and take as big a bite as you can manage. Then, as the piping hot juice and fat run down your face, you quickly wipe your chin on the sleeve of your coat to avoid being scarred for life.

'A pickled egg is regarded as sophisticated in Scotland.'

STEPHEN OLIVER

THE BRIDIE

A bridie is a Scottish pasty, first made by bakers in Forfar more than 150 years ago. The name is sometimes said to come from bridies having been served at weddings, although not many modern Scottish brides would thank you for suggesting that the humble bridie should be served on their big day. Another theory is that it is named after Margaret Bridie of Glamis, whose bridies were much sought after in the market at Forfar.

So what is a bridie? It can't really be accurately compared with any kind of English pasty because, in typical Scots fashion, there are no vegetables to be found in a bridie, apart from onion, and not always even that. The bridie is made from a large oval of shortcrust pastry. A filling of minced steak, butter and suet, with lots of salt and pepper, is placed on one half of the oval. The other half is then folded over the top and the edges are crimped together. Before it goes in the oven, the baker marks the bridie with one hole in the top if it has no onion – a plain bridie – and two holes if it is an onion bridie.

THE DOCTOR'S APOLOGY

Former *Doctor Who* star David Tennant had to make a humble apology after maligning one of Scotland's great breakfast components – the square sausage. In an interview in the United States, he said, 'We have this strange thing called the square sausage in Scotland,' and went on to describe how he reckoned the square or lorne sausage was made from meat that wasn't good enough for regular sausages. He described it as meat that had been scraped off the floor of the butcher's shop and slapped into a

flat, tile shape. 'In fact,' he said, 'you could probably tile your bathroom with them and they would be entirely impregnable to everything.'

Scottish butchers were outraged that their favourite Doctor could be so scathing about their lovely square sausages, which are most definitely not made with floor scrapings. Tennant issued a profuse apology, admitting that he was only trying to raise a laugh and that he actually really liked the square sausage, confessing that, as a Scot in exile, 'I do miss it.'

SQUARE SAUSAGE WITH A DIFFERENCE

If David Tennant is really keen to get his teeth into some square sausage again, then he might also like to try a slightly different kind. It's still square, but you wouldn't want to fry or grill it because it's ice cream.

In July 2018, a Scottish dairy firm prepared the dessert for National Ice Cream day at the Grassmarket Hotel in Edinburgh. The sausage was sourced from a top butcher before being cooked, grated and added to the ice-cream mix. It was then served as a square slice inside a brioche bun that was toasted and dusted with icing sugar. For the final touch of what was made to look very much like breakfast fare, brown sauce was added, dribbling out of the bun. It was actually brown toffee drizzle, but it gave the dish the unmistakable appearance of a square sausage in a morning roll.

'My theory is that all of Scottish cuisine is
based on a dare.'

MIKE MYERS

CULLEN SKINK

It sounds like something you'd be glad you didn't stand in and, indeed, you certainly wouldn't want to do that because Cullen skink is a delicious soup. Made from smoked haddock, potatoes and onions, with milk or cream sometimes also being used, it graces the menu at top restaurants throughout Scotland. The name comes, at least in part, from Cullen in north-east Scotland where the dish originated. A skink is a kind of lizard, so how did that get in there? Don't worry, as in the Scots language 'skink' means 'soup made from shin of beef' and more recently the word has come to mean a soup or broth. No reptiles are harmed in the making of Cullen skink.

'This lamb is so undercooked, it's following
Mary to school!'

GORDON RAMSAY IN *HELL'S KITCHEN*

THE GREAT PIE BAN

Who would want to ban a pie. It's a staple of the Scottish diet and surely a Scotch pie once in a wee while can't do you too much harm? Maybe not, but how about a fry-up breakfast pie stuffed with sausage, bacon, black pudding and beans, and with a fried egg nestling invitingly on the top? The breakfast pie became a bestseller at bakeries throughout Dundee from around 2014, but the reason that the 800-calorie delight came under threat of a ban was because the snack that health professionals described as 'a heart attack on a plate' was being sold in Ninewells Hospital.

> 'Some place Govan, eh? Where else can you get a fish supper at 9 a.m.? Simple, just steal it off a drunk that's been lying pished outside a close all night.'
>
> RAB C. NESBITT

SHORTIE

No, it's not an insult for someone who is vertically challenged. Well, it is, but it is also one of Scotland's most famous foods, exported in tartan tins all over the world – shortbread. The sweet, buttery biscuits come in all shapes and sizes, from fingers and triangles to rounds and unidentifiable flower moulds. It is one of the three things traditionally carried by a man going 'first-footing' at Hogmanay (New Year's Eve). The idea is that the man, who will be the first to cross the threshold on New Year's Day – hence 'first-footing' – will bring luck to the household if he is tall, dark and handsome (no shorties here), and brings a lump of coal, an offering of food and whisky. The coal means that there will be fuel for the fire all year; the food, which is usually shortie, means that there will be food all year; and the whisky means that nobody cares if he forgot the other two things.

THE MYSTERIOUS HAGGIS

You can't talk about Scottish food without mentioning haggis. For years the Scots have delighted in telling anyone who asked that the haggis is a small Highland animal, rarely seen, and that there are two types. One type of haggis has two left legs shorter than those on the right, the other has two shorter right legs. Why? Because one runs around the mountain clockwise and the other anti-clockwise. Stories like that have been going on for so long that nobody asks any more.

Haggis is, of course, a savoury pudding made from the minced heart, liver and lungs of a sheep mixed with oatmeal, suet, spices, stock and salt, all stuffed into a sheep's stomach. Now you probably wished you'd stuck with the short-leggie story. These days an artificial sausage skin is normally used instead of the sheep's stomach. Does that sound any better?

Served hot, and piped into the dining room at formal dinners by a bagpiper, haggis is traditionally accompanied by mashed neeps (turnip) and mashed tatties (potatoes) and whisky. The haggis is ceremonially cut open following a recitation of Robert Burns' poem 'Address to a Haggis'.

ADDRESS TO A HAGGIS
WHAT IT ALL MEANS

Fair fa' your honest, sonsie face,
Good fortune to you and your honest, plump face
Great chieftain o the puddin'-race!
High king of sausage puddings
Aboon them a' ye tak your place,
You are above all other sausage puddings
Painch, tripe, or thairm:
Stomach, tripe or intestines
Weel are ye worthy o' a grace
You deserve a tribute
As lang's my arm.
As long as my arm

HAGGIS AT BAY

And, indeed, the address goes on for another seven verses. It's a wonderful poem but, given that the person reciting it will have an audience of Scots anxious to get stuck into their haggis, tatties, neeps – and did I mention whisky? – it is occasionally cut short. Very short. Just the first verse.

Burns also wrote 'To a Mouse', but he never got a reply.

AND FOR AFTERS …

At a Burns Supper, held to celebrate the Scottish bard's birthday on 25 January, once you have tucked away as much haggis, tatties and neeps as you can manage, you may be served the delicious Cranachan as dessert.

After the far heavier, but still scrumptious, haggis course, Cranachan comes as a marvellously refreshing follow-up. Usually served in a glass rather than a bowl in order that you can appreciate the fresh fruit colours, Cranachan is a mixture of raspberries, whipped cream, honey, whisky and roasted oats.

I suppose it goes without saying that it is traditionally served with a glass of whisky, which some like to pour over the top. Burns, who enjoyed a dram or two, would certainly have approved.

THE NOBLE BLACK BUN

Robert Louis Stevenson apparently described it as 'a black substance inimical to life', but he was generally so ill that, for him, pretty much everything was probably 'inimical to life'. How could you not like a fruit cake packed with raisins, currants, nuts, orange peel, ginger and cinnamon and then wrapped in a pastry case? It's like a cake in a pie – so Scottish that it practically swears at you.

Black bun has a noble history, too. Like shortbread and Dundee cake it was a favourite of Mary, Queen of Scots and, also like shortbread, became a traditional gift for the host when 'first-footing' at Hogmanay. Strangely, it may also have been the inspiration for the Garibaldi biscuit. The biscuit was named in honour of an Italian general, Giuseppe Garibaldi, who visited Britain in 1854. The biscuit was made by Peek, Frean & Co. in London, the recipe having been devised by their Scottish baker, John Carr.

So here we have a cake in a pie that inspired a biscuit named after an Italian and produced in England by a Scotsman. You can't deny that Scottish cuisine has an international flavour!

A SPECIAL TREAT

An Aberdonian and his wife were walking through the centre of town when they passed a restaurant. A wonderful cooking aroma filled the air.

'Doesn't that smell lovely?' said his wife.

'Aye, it does that,' said the husband and, feeling his heart soften, he decided to give his wife a treat.

So he walked her past the restaurant again.

'A girl once came to my beery flat in Kensal Green, opened the blinds and cooked me breakfast. I married her.'

PETER CAPALDI

IT'S MACAROON, NOT MACARON

In Paris, every patisserie you pass will tempt you with dainty, colourful macarons that melt in the mouth. In Glasgow, and throughout Scotland, you will find a sweet treat of an entirely different nature – the macaroon bar. It is neither light, dainty nor particularly colourful, and would struggle to melt in the mouth of one of Daenerys Targaryen's dragons – but it is delicious.

The macaroon bar was invented by Coatbridge confectioner John J. Lees when he was trying to devise a smooth fondant filling for a chocolate bar. His idea was to base his fondant on lots of sugar and that unlikely but very Scottish ingredient, mashed potato. The fondant didn't really work out, but what he did have was a firm filling, incredibly sweet, that he dipped in chocolate and covered in toasted coconut. That was in 1931 and Scottish dentists have been in Mr Lees' debt ever since …

SALT 'N' SAUCE

In other parts of the UK, when you're standing at the counter in the chip shop watching your steaming hot chips being shovelled out of the drainer above the deep-fat fryer, your server will doubtless ask, 'Salt 'n' vinegar?' In Scotland, you are just as likely to hear 'Salt 'n' sauce?'

Karen Gillan, the Inverness-born former model and *Doctor Who* companion, spends a great deal of her time nowadays in exile. Her career has moved on since her time-travelling days in the Tardis as Amy Pond and she is more likely to be found in the United States and attending glitzy showbiz parties and previews than she is dodging Daleks. She admits to missing her family back in Inverness but also confesses that, 'The thing I miss most about Scotland has to be the chippy sauce!'

So what is Scotland's celebrated condiment? Essentially, chippy sauce is brown sauce, which is made to a number of different, highly secret recipes that generally include tomatoes, fruit, spices and vinegar. To turn brown sauce into chippy sauce, it is diluted with more vinegar or even water.

Serve over a poke of hot chips and eat while you're waiting for the last bus home!

'Most traditional Scottish food is designed to use things that are just about to go off.'

SCOTT HUTCHISON

THE SCOTTISH DIET

Two American tourists were in Crieff enjoying a luxury break at the Crieff Hydro spa hotel and decided to go for a walk. On the outskirts of town they came across a small, wizened man sitting on a wall in the sunshine smoking a pipe. The man bade them a cheerful 'Good morning' and they stopped for a chat. One of the tourists said how impressed they were with his cheerfulness and asked what his recipe was for a long, happy life.

'I smoke forty fags a day,' said the local. 'Plus an ounce or two of tobacco. I drink a bottle of whisky and ten pints of beer, I never eat vegetables and anything I do eat has to be fried in fat.'

'That's remarkable,' said the tourist. 'How old are you?'

'Twenty-four,' said the local.

'If the Good Lord had wanted us to know about cuisine, he would never have given us crispy pancakes.'

RAB C. NESBITT

THE BUTTERY

If you like your bread hard, fatty and salty, the buttery is for you. These delicious bread rolls come from Aberdeen where they were made so that fishermen could have bread that wouldn't go stale when they'd been out at sea for two weeks. The high fat content also means that they are good fuel for working men, giving them lots of energy.

Today, butteries are served in restaurants or tea shops. They give you jam and butter to spread on them, but legend has it that in Scottish tea shops they heat up the knives so that the customers can't use too much butter . . .

'Oats. A grain, which in England is generally given to horses, but in Scotland supports the people.'

SAMUEL JOHNSON

CHAPTER NINE

WHAT DID HE SAY?

You might be forgiven for thinking that Gaelic is the traditional, historic language of the people of Scotland, but you wouldn't be forgiven by most of us. We don't speak Gaelic and we don't really want to. Only a little over one per cent of Scotland's population speaks Gaelic and many of them, although they might be loath to admit it, are not actually fluent. The majority of people in Scotland think that Gaelic sounds charmingly poetic and that it is a beautiful language which should be learned, nurtured, cherished and preserved . . . by somebody else.

TAXI PROTOCOL

I happen to know from personal experience what it is like for an English visitor to Dundee coming up against a broad Dundonian accent for the first time because I once took a young lady there. To paraphrase Charlotte Brontë, Reader, I married her.

We walked to a taxi rank in the Nethergate in the city centre where a line of taxis stood one behind the other. As it was fine weather, all of the drivers were standing by the driver's-side door of their cars, chatting loudly. Seeing that there was nobody queueing she walked towards the nearest car and was stopped in her tracks when the driver smiled and said, 'Goannaetakafrontane, hen?'

You can probably work out from the glossary below that what he was saying was, 'Would you mind taking the front one, my dear?'

Someone then did take the front taxi and my future wife was astonished to see that, rather than starting their engines, to save petrol the taxi drivers all pushed their cars forward one space! She may have found it all quite outlandish, but I immediately knew that I was back home – a language indecipherable to outsiders and back-breaking frugality!

GLOSSARY

A

a'	all
an'	and
an a'	as well, too
ane	one
auld	old
awa	away
awfy	awful
aye	yes

B

bahoochie	bottom or buttocks
bairn	a child
bampot	someone of unsound mind or with no understanding of what is socially acceptable
bannock	an oatmeal biscuit
baltic	very cold
bawheid	a bald person or eejit
belter	an attractive woman or wonderful thing
bide	stay or reside
bile	boil
birl	spin
blether	inane chatter

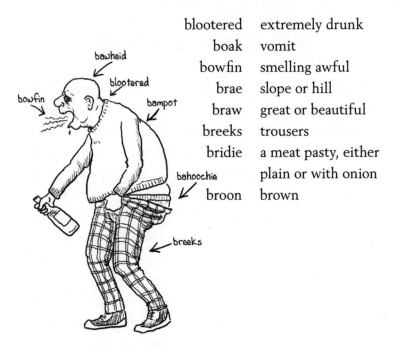

blootered	extremely drunk
boak	vomit
bowfin	smelling awful
brae	slope or hill
braw	great or beautiful
breeks	trousers
bridie	a meat pasty, either plain or with onion
broon	brown

Some words in context, when having been persuaded to wear light trousers during frosty weather:
My bahoochie's pure baltic in these breeks, ye bampot.
These trousers aren't keeping me very warm.

C

cannae	cannot
cauld	cold
chanty	a potty or chamber pot
cloot	cloth
coo	a cow
crackin'	very good, outstanding
cundie	a drain at the side of the road

PARLIAMO GLASGOW

Comedian Stanley Baxter created a much-loved sketch sequence as part of his long-running series of TV shows during the 1960s and 1970s – 'Parliamo Glasgow'. In the sketches Baxter and his collaborators created a spoof educational segment inviting the viewers to learn Glaswegian as though it were a foreign language, which to many, of course, it is.

They would play out a scene in aggressively loud Glaswegian accents, pause, then break to address the viewer in impeccable BBC English to point out the way that words and phrases were used. Baxter invented phrases that were so acutely close to the way that people really spoke that they ended up being adopted by viewers in Scotland and worked their way into everyday speech, having fun with words and helping the language to evolve.

Some of the phrases he used included:

Sootra – meaning 'is out of'. To be used when someone is facing into a room and sitting against the window ledge, as in 'Yer bum sootra windie!'

Sanawfy – meaning 'it's an awful'. To be used, perhaps, when the weather turns chilly, as in 'Sanawfy cauld day.'

Izziaffiz – meaning 'is he off his'. To be used when asking whether someone has lost his appetite or perhaps even lost his mind, as in 'Izziaffiz meat?' or 'Izziaffiz heid?'

D

dae	do
dead	very
deid	dead
dinnae	do not
doolally	unstable or deranged
doon	down
dour	miserable
dram	a shot of whisky
dreich	damp weather
dunderhead	see 'eejit'
dunt	bump

E

eejit	someone with a low IQ
erse	see 'bahoochie'

F

fae	from
feart	afraid
fidget	to squirm or make small annoying movements
firth	estuary

Some words in context, when advising someone whose boss is upset with them:
Dinnae be feart an' tell him tae awa an' bile his heid.
Try not to be frightened and stand up for yourself.

THE BEST SPOKEN ENGLISH

In Scotland we can be proud of just about anything we claim to be Scottish, and we can claim just about anything to be Scottish, so we are pretty much proud of everything, especially the fact that it has long been accepted that the best spoken English you can hope to hear will be in the north of Perthshire or the Highland Region around Inverness.

Sean Connery, one of Scotland's greatest exports, had a voice and pronunciation that helped to make him an international 'shoopershtar', so he knows a thing or two about diction. 'When you hear someone from the very north of Scotland speaking,' he said, 'I think it's nice, very musical and harmonious.' The theory is that the area in the north-west of Scotland and the Western Isles has always been the place where Gaelic was the first language and that people learned to speak very precisely, enunciating perfectly every vowel and consonant.

We can also be proud of the fact that Scots may well also speak the worst English. One commentator on social media observed that in 'central Scotland we have the reserved ones. Go north, we have the backwards Fifers. Further north, the unintelligible Dundonians.'

G

gie	give
gies	give us or give me
glaikit	the demeanour of an eejit

gloaming	dusk
gonnae	are you going to or would you mind
greet	to cry
greetin' face	a sad-looking person

H

hackit	not pretty
haud	hold
havers	fibs or general nonsensical talk
heid	head
hen	affectionate term for a woman
hingin	hanging
hoachin	extremely busy
hoo	how
how	why
howkin	lifting, throwing or picking

I

ingin	onion
intae	into
isnae	isn't

Some words in context when at the bakery:

Gonnae gies twa plen bridies an' an ingin ane an a'?

May I please have two plain bridies and an onion one as well?

GONNAE NO DAE THAT

Chewin' the Fat was a BBC Scotland sketch show that started out on radio and, between 1999 and 2002, enjoyed four series on TV. The show introduced a host of characters, some of whom continued in spin-off series, and a number of catchphrases that became part of everyday language. One of these was 'Gonnae no dae that?' Two bored lighthouse keepers isolated on a remote 'Aonoch Mor' lighthouse in 1901, one a practical joker and the other the long-suffering target of his pranks, had the same exchange after each increasingly involved gag:

Gonnae no dae that?

(translates as) Would you mind not doing that?

How?

(translates as) Why?

Just gonnae no!

(translates as) Just don't!

The phrase became so popular that there is now a thriving ice-cream parlour in Airdrie called Coney No Dae That.

J

jessie	a camp man
jobby	excrement

K

keech	see 'jobby'
keek	a glimpse
keeker	a black eye
ken	know or understand
kerry	carry
kerry oot	takeaway drink or food

L

laldie	maximum effort
lang	long
lumber	spouse or partner

Some words in context down on the farm:
Me an' the lumber gied it laldie at the tattie howkin. It was hoachin.
My wife and I worked hard picking potatoes as there was a lot to do.

CENTRAL HEATING

On a cold morning in Glasgow, a woman walked into her local butcher's shop to see him standing with his hands behind his back, leaning forward slightly and enjoying the heat from a small electric fire. The woman runs her eye over the meat counter and says, 'Is that yer Ayrshire bacon?'

'No,' says the butcher. 'I'm just warming ma hands.'

'A lot of people say that it's a lack of vocabulary that makes you swear. Rubbish. I know thousands of words but I still prefer f**k!'

BILLY CONNOLLY

M

mackle	large amount
mak	make
manky	filthy
mickle	small amount
mince	nonsense or rubbish
mind	remember or look out for
mingin	smelly, revolting, drunk or all three

Some words in context in an old Scottish proverb:
Many a mickle maks a muckle.
Lots of small things generally combine to create something larger.

N

napper	see 'heid'
naw	no
neeps	turnips
nip	see 'dram'
no	not
noo	now
numpty	an unintentional eejit

O

oot	out
oxter	an armpit

COMMUNICATIONS BREAKDOWN

American actor Michael Keaton had more than a little trouble communicating with the locals on one trip to Glasgow. He described the way that most people there spoke, the real Glaswegian accent, as 'making Billy Connolly sound like he comes from Cincinnati'. Having picked up a hire car at the airport, Keaton wasn't having much luck in driving to his hotel and, in the gathering gloom of late evening, he decided to stop and ask for directions. Spotting one local weaving along the pavement, he pulled over and asked the way to the hotel. The local gave him a long and intricate explanation of how to get there, but in such a thick, and somewhat slurred, Glaswegian accent that

Keaton couldn't understand a word of it. After a couple of requests for clarification, he eventually beckoned the man into the car so that he could simply show him the way. The man manoeuvred himself into the car and directed Keaton through the city with what sounded to him like a series of burbling grunts, but also with some useful pointing.

Eventually, the man signalled to Keaton to stop, although the hotel was still nowhere in sight. 'He got out and said, "Thanks",' said Keaton. 'He had taken me to his own house!'

CARELESS WORDS

Mrs Morrison in Perth couldn't wait to meet her new neighbours, the Patersons, when they moved in next door. She watched their furniture being unloaded from the removal van and it all looked far better than hers. She saw the men carrying in a TV that was far bigger than hers. Then the Patersons arrived in a car that was far more expensive than hers. Naturally, she went out to greet them and was hugely impressed with how posh they were. Showing the spirit of a good neighbour, she invited them to tea.

Mrs Morrison then embarked on panicked preparations for her guests. She taught her daughter to say grace, then rushed around cleaning the house, baking a sponge and scones, and laying out the best china.

When the neighbours arrived and were seated at the table in the front room, Mrs Morrison asked her daughter to say grace. The little girl stared at her blankly.

'Go on,' said her mother. 'Just say what I said earlier, starting with "Dear God" ...'

'Dear God,' said the little girl, 'why the hell did I invite those pan-loafy Patersons round to tea ...'

P

palaver	fuss
pan-loafy	snooty or posh – bread was either plain or pan-baked, but a pan loaf was more expensive
peely-wally	pale skinned or feeble-looking
piece	a sandwich
plen	plain
polis	a police officer
puggled	exhausted
pure	absolutely

R

rammy	a vigorous brawl
ran-dan	an evening of vigorous refreshment

S

scrieve	to write
skelp	slap
stoater	see 'belter'
stocious	see 'blootered'
stookie	a plaster cast on a broken limb
swally	a drink
syne	since

T

tak	take
tattie	potato
teuchter	yokel
thon	that
toon	town
twa	two

U

urnae	are not

W

wabbit	see 'puggled'
wallies	dentures
wee	small
whaur	where
wheesht	quiet
wi'	with
wifie	an old woman

Y

yon	over there or yonder
yonks	a very long period of time

Some words in context from a government propaganda poster:

Haud yer wheesht an' get on wi' it.

Keep calm and carry on.

TOO TRENDY TOTS

You have to be careful when you try to use trendy language. A story circulated recently about three friends from a Glasgow primary school, thick as thieves and as mischievous as only young boys can be. They decided to boost their street cred with cool nicknames. Ryan told everyone to call him Rydo, Alan told everyone to call him Aldo, and Dylan couldn't understand why everyone was laughing at him.

'There is no such thing as too much swearing.
Swearing is just a piece of linguistic mechanics.
The words in-between are the clever ones.'

PETER CAPALDI

CHAPTER TEN

THE WATER OF LIFE

Whisky is famous as the national drink of Scotland and achieving that status is no mean feat, given the competition that it's up against. The Scots, after all, are famous for drinking just about anything they can lay their hands on. Of course, we're not all raging alcoholics, but there's no denying the drinking culture in Scotland. Having such a close association with whisky, and other good drinks, the Scots are also no strangers to drunken pranks, memory blanks and the inevitable hangovers, as the stories below ably demonstrate.

KEEP IT CONEY

In Glasgow's Royal Exchange Square there is a statue of the Duke of Wellington, mounted on a horse and towering above the square. 'That's not so unusual,' you might think, 'there are statues of the Iron Duke all over the country.' The Glasgow statue, however, is slightly different. The duke wears an orange-and-white traffic cone on his head.

The cone first appeared in the 1980s, placed there one night by drunken pranksters. The local council removed it. The sozzled midnight cone fiends replaced it. Every time the council relieved the duke of his burden, the cone was back again within a couple of days and the statue became known as 'Coneheid'.

Then, in 2013, the council, who estimated that repeatedly removing the cone was costing around £10,000 a year, proposed raising the height of the plinth on which the statue stands in order to deter the dangerous practice of drunks climbing it at night to pop a cone on the duke's head. Sometimes his horse got one, too, and was known as 'the Scottish unicorn'.

The plinth project would have cost around £65,000, but cone fans objected to such a sum being spent. The obvious solution was simply to leave the cone where it was. A campaign was launched and 72,000 people signed a 'save the cone' petition. Amazingly, the council gave in.

Nowadays, the duke retains his cone and remains otherwise unmolested, although one year a drunken Santa Claus who tied himself to the duke to ride pillion and sing songs had to be persuaded to dismount by firemen with a ladder. Coneheid is now a tourist attraction. Indeed, a replica of the statue, complete with traffic cone, was part of the opening ceremony of the Glasgow 2014 Commonwealth Games, and 'Keep it Coney' has become an accepted term for always being prepared to have a giggle no matter what life throws at you.

'Love makes the world go round? Not at all. Whisky makes it go round twice as fast.'

COMPTON MACKENZIE

DRINKING SHORTS

A young boy walked into a pub in Edinburgh to a hushed silence from the regular drinkers. Children were generally neither expected, welcome nor even tolerated in the establishment. With all eyes upon him, he strode confidently up to the bar, reached up to slap his hands on the counter and said with great confidence in his mousey, nine-year-old voice: 'Whisky, please. Make it a double.'

'You'll get me into trouble,' said the barmaid.

'Maybe later,' said the boy. 'Let's have that drink first.'

'A well-balanced person has a drink in each hand.'

BILLY CONNOLLY

*'Inhabiting a small impoverished country ridged by
bleak mountains and ringed by rocky coasts against
which rough seas sweep and surge, the Scots are hardy,
frugal, thrifty, resolute and addicted to "usquebaugh", a
Gaelic word vilely corrupted by the Saxons to "whisky".'*

A. J. CRONIN

PORTLAND'S HONORARY SCOT

Brian Kidd was born in Virginia in the United States and if
he hasn't already been given honorary Scots status it should
be conferred upon him without delay. He's a clever
lad, having studied marine biology at the University
of Virginia before making his home in Portland,
Oregon. It was in Virginia that he found a
unicycle in a skip, deciding to repair it and
learn to ride it.

This he did, which is a skill in itself,
displaying admirable Scottish frugality, but
after a few drinks one night, Brian's friends
challenged him to combine unicycling with
his other hobby – playing the bagpipes.
After a few attempts in a deserted car park,

Brian was up and running, but the thing that has really earned him the right to Scottishness was when videos of him went viral in 2011. He was unicycling while dressed in kilt and a Darth Vader mask and playing 'The Imperial March' (Darth Vader's theme) on his bagpipes. And the pipes were spouting flames.

It's amazing what can be achieved with the encouragement of a few drinks.

'The man that takes a good drink, he's a man. When ye're teetotal … ach! When ye're teetotal ye've always got a rotten feeling that everybody's your boss.'

WILL FYFFE

DRINK AND THE DEVIL

A Salvation Army band was playing outside a hostelry in Dunfermline when Billy MacGregor strolled up to the door.

'If you go in there,' warned a female Salvationist, shaking her tambourine at Billy, 'the Devil is at your shoulder.'

'Is that so?' said Billy. 'Well, tell him it's his round and mine's a dram.'

'The Glasgow invention of square-toed shoes was to enable the Glasgow man to get closer to the bar.'

JACK HOUSE

'I did smoke pot a few times but nothing else. I would never inject. I'm too fond of the drink. At times I can go two weeks or more without it, but then I'm quite enthusiastic to get back to the taste again.'

SEAN CONNERY

HOW TO AVOID DRINKING AND DRIVING

Getting home in the wee small hours after a party can be a problem. After you've had a few drams, everyone knows that you should never get in your car and drive. That would be madness. Taxis can sometimes be hard to come by as well, especially on New Year's Day, the morning after the Hogmanay celebrations. Even the following morning, of course, when you've had a few hours' sleep, you can easily still be well over the legal limit for driving. One Dundee motorist – entirely sober – was driving along a dual carriageway in the early hours of New Year's Day in 2015, approaching an underpass, when he saw a police car up ahead that had clearly stopped a vehicle on the road. There were no footpaths nearby and the motorist carefully pulled out to pass the police car. When he glanced over to see what was going on he could hardly believe his eyes. The road user the police officers had pulled over was a man mounted on a large, orange spacehopper!

PRICELESS . . .

A tourist couple visiting Aberdeen were attracted to a pub in the city centre where a crowd of people were queueing outside, chatting, reading newspapers and waiting patiently in line. Then they spotted a sign on the pavement at the head of the queue that said, 'Centenary opening celebrations – rolling back the years. All beer two pence a pint.'

The pub appeared to be open, so the couple wandered in to find the barman polishing glasses in the empty bar.

'Are you actually open for business?' they asked

'Aye,' said the barman. 'We are that.'

'So why is there a queue outside?' asked the tourists. 'Surely the locals will want to take advantage of these prices.'

'I'm sure you're right,' said the barman, 'but they're waiting for the Happy Hour.'

'I'm now on a banana and seaweed diet. It hasn't improved my football but I'm a helluva better swimmer.'

GORDON STRACHAN

HATS OFF TO THE QUEEN MOTHER

The Queen Mother was well known for enjoying the odd tipple. For many years her favourite was gin and Dubonnet, which simply had to be mixed with two parts Dubonnet to one part gin. She had a very positive, Scottish attitude to life, as was revealed by a quotation cited in William Shawcross' book, *Queen Elizabeth The Queen Mother: The Official Biography*, which was published in 2009, seven years after the Queen Mother died at the ripe old age of 101. 'Wouldn't it be terrible if you'd spent all your life doing everything you were supposed to do, didn't drink, didn't smoke, didn't eat things, took lots of exercise, all the things you didn't want to do . . . ' she is quoted as having said, '. . . and suddenly one day you were run over by a big red bus, and as the wheels were crunching into you you'd say "Oh my God, I could have got so drunk last night!"'

That would indeed have been a terrible way to go, but the Queen Mother took certain precautions to ensure that this would never be her fate. When she was away from home on lengthy official trips, rather than anyone spotting an overloaded carrier bag or hearing the tell-tale clink of bottles as her gin and Dubonnet supplies were loaded or unloaded between transport and accommodation, she elegantly concealed them in hat boxes, excusing herself by saying that she 'couldn't get through all my royal engagements without a little something'.

> *'One more drink and I'll be under the host.'*
> DOROTHY PARKER (HER MOTHER WAS SCOTTISH)

HAIR OF THE DOG

You know you've got a hangover when you wake up and go to brush something off your shoulder and realize that it's the floor. Then the dog licks your face and you think, 'Hang on a minute, I don't have a dog . . .'

Then the hangover symptoms start. In Scotland there has long been a story about the bad bear that visits you during the night while you're asleep. He eats all the food in your fridge, drinks all your booze, wrecks your living room, scatters your clothes all over the floor and then craps in your mouth.

Once you start suffering the full-blown hangover symptoms – dizziness, a pounding headache, dehydration, upset stomach and an intolerance to either bright lights or loud noises – you really need to do something about it. In Scotland that generally means taking a 'hair of the dog' – another beer, another whisky or another of whatever it was that got you into this state in the first place. Ever wondered about that phrase 'hair of the dog'? It comes from an ancient remedy for rabies. If you were bitten by a mad dog, the idea was that you would pluck a hair from the tail of the dog, presumably after it had been subdued unless you wanted another savaging, and then burn the hair. You then crushed the ash into a drink, or ate it, or sprinkled it onto the wound to ward off rabies.

It is, of course, far simpler just to get yourself down to the pub, completely ignoring all dogs, order yourself a drink, then order another drink and keep doing so until your hangover is cured or you simply don't care anymore. Better still, get someone else to order the drinks ...

'I'm on a whisky diet. I've lost three days already.'

TOMMY COOPER

BLOOTERED ON BUCKFAST

One of the most unusual drinks consumed in Scotland is Buckfast Tonic Wine. On first reading, you might think that sounds a bit like a health drink, but don't be fooled by its innocent disguise. Neither should you let the fact that it is produced by mild-mannered Benedictine monks at Buckfast Abbey in peaceful Devon sway you towards the opinion that this is a harmless tipple.

Its alcohol content is only 15 per cent, which is strong for wine but not outrageous when compared to whisky, which is 40 per cent. Buckfast does, however, have a high caffeine content as well as containing lots of sugar and other goodies that combine to get Buckfast fans truly blootered in no time at all.

Buckfast is not popular all over Scotland but seems to

"Buckie"... lose the heid

be concentrated in an area around Glasgow that takes in Airdrie, Coatbridge and Cumbernauld, which has become known as the 'Buckie Triangle'. Strathclyde Police deal with up to eight Buckfast-related crimes every day, ranging from petty offences to serious assaults and even murder. Buckfast has a peculiar effect on drinkers who can tend to 'lose the heid' completely rather than simply enjoying a relaxing social drink with friends, turning into wild creatures who smash ornaments, break windows and destroy furniture – which is why the drink has been nicknamed 'Wreck the hoose juice'.

'Hangover – the wrath of grapes.'

DOROTHY PARKER

153

McGONAGALL – THE DEMON DRINK

Although you could scarcely tell it from the poetry he wrote, William Topaz McGonagall, the Worst Poet in the World, was a teetotaller and an ardent campaigner for abstinence. His poem 'The Demon Drink' ran to sixteen verses, but the first five are the wisest and, unknown to poor William, also the funniest:

Oh, thou demon Drink, thou fell destroyer;
Thou curse of society, and its greatest annoyer.
What hast thou done to society, let me think?

I answer thou hast caused the most of ills, thou
*   demon Drink.*

Thou causeth the mother to neglect her child,
Also the father to act as he were wild,
So that he neglects his loving wife and family dear,
By spending his earnings foolishly on whisky, rum
*   and beer.*

And after spending his earnings foolishly he beats his wife–
The man that promised to protect her during life–
And so the man would if there was no drink in society,
For seldom a man beats his wife in a state of sobriety.

And if he does, perhaps he finds his wife fou',
Then that causes, no doubt, a great hullaballo;
When he finds his wife drunk he begins to frown,
And in a fury of passion he knocks her down.

And in that knock down she fractures her head,
And perhaps the poor wife she is killed dead,
Whereas, if there was no strong drink to be got,
To be killed wouldn't have been the poor wife's lot.

'We would have injected vitamin C if only
they had made it illegal.'

MARK RENTON IN *TRAINSPOTTING* (1996)

CURING THE COMMON COLD

There are many supposed cures for the common cold but scientists have yet to find a definitive remedy. Sir Alexander Fleming, the Scottish physician, microbiologist and pharmacologist, is a man of whom the Scots are extremely proud. Among his many achievements was the discovery of penicillin. In a poll organized by Scottish Television, viewers voted him the third 'Greatest Scot' of all time, with only Rabbie Burns and Sir William Wallace above him on the list.

As a medical man, his advice for dealing with the common cold was simple: 'A good gulp of whisky at bedtime – it's not very scientific, but it helps.'

'Whisky is liquid sunshine.'
GEORGE BERNARD SHAW

THE GROUSE CAKE

This might well be one of Scotland's favourite delicacies – no one really knows. No one has ever tasted it. If you follow the recipe, you will find out why!

Ingredients

6 ounces of butter
1 cup of water
1 cup of white sugar
1 cup of brown sugar
6 eggs
1 teaspoon of baking soda
1 teaspoon of salt
A handful of sultanas

A handful of dried cherries
A handful of raspberries
1 bottle of The Famous Grouse whisky

Method

First, open the bottle of Grouse. Try a large glass to check that it's fresh. It will be, but best be on the safe side.

Fetch a large bowl from the cupboard to mix your cake mixture and have another wee Grouse to keep you going.

Find your electric mixer which will not be in the place where you last left it because nothing ever is around here, is it? People borrow stuff and move stuff without even asking. Taking liberties, that's what it is!

Have another dram to calm yourself down.

Repeat.

Beat the butter in the bowl until you are light and fluffy, then add the sugar and salt and beat it. When you get back (ha-ha – that was just a wee joke there!), egg your cracks into the bowl and zoosh it all around with the merxer.

Try another dram. You deserve it.

Chuck the fruit in the bowlie and try not to stuck it all in your mixering as you're quite thick. Then get that salt or whatever and your sugars if you can be bothered. It's a real pain. Who cares anyway?

Check the Grouse again to make sure it's at toom remprature.

Add whatever you've got left, or whatever else you like. Have another dram and on no account switch on the oven at gas mark sick. You're not troo be tusted with that.

Turn out your mixture upside down into the bin. Best place for it. Job well done. Have another Grouse and go to bed, you must be knackered.

'There are two rules for drinking whisky. First, never take whisky without water, and second, never take water without whisky.'

CHIC MURRAY

---

*'I should never have switched from
Scotch to Martinis.'*

REPUTED TO BE THE
LAST WORDS OF ACTOR HUMPHREY BOGART